Building Trust between Faculty and Administrators

In this unique and timely book, Dr. Lisa B. Fiore and Dr. Catherine Koverola explore and illuminate the tensions between faculty and administrators that have become ubiquitous in higher education and which cause conflicts that may adversely affect students and the institution. The authors harness their extensive professional expertise in cross-cultural communication and education, their years of personal experience working through conflicts in higher education, and their collaborative research to provide a guide for building trust and productive relationships.

With an approach anchored in intercultural theory and practice, the authors lay a foundation upon which readers can build new understanding about the "other" constituents with whom they work. Practical tools such as case studies, sample scripts, discussion points, and resources will resonate with faculty and administrators at colleges and universities, as well as aspiring higher education practitioners.

Readers will immediately recognize universal themes and scenarios and will appreciate the authors' straightforward approach that will translate into tangible, meaningful changes in their professional relationships. This book moves discussions forward, from argumentation and resentment to positive behavior change that grows from a place of trust and mutual respect.

Lisa B. Fiore is Professor of Education and Chair of the Department of Education, and Director of the Child Homelessness Initiative at Lesley University, USA.

Catherine Koverola is Professor of Psychology at the University of Pittsburgh at Bradford and Titusville, USA, and has previously served in the roles of dean, provost, and president at institutions of higher education.

Building Trust between Faculty and Administrators

An Intercultural Perspective

Lisa B. Fiore
Catherine Koverola

Routledge
Taylor & Francis Group
NEW YORK AND LONDON

Cover Image: © Getty Images

First published 2022
by Routledge
605 Third Avenue, New York, NY 10158

and by Routledge
2 Park Square, Milton Park, Abingdon, Oxon, OX14 4RN

Routledge is an imprint of the Taylor & Francis Group, an informa business

© 2022 Lisa B. Fiore and Catherine Koverola

The right of Lisa B. Fiore and Catherine Koverola to be identified as authors of this work has been asserted by them in accordance with sections 77 and 78 of the Copyright, Designs and Patents Act 1988.

All rights reserved. No part of this book may be reprinted or reproduced or utilised in any form or by any electronic, mechanical, or other means, now known or hereafter invented, including photocopying and recording, or in any information storage or retrieval system, without permission in writing from the publishers.

Trademark notice: Product or corporate names may be trademarks or registered trademarks, and are used only for identification and explanation without intent to infringe.

Library of Congress Cataloging-in-Publication Data
A catalog record for this title has been requested

ISBN: 978-0-367-70966-2 (hbk)
ISBN: 978-0-367-70965-5 (pbk)
ISBN: 978-1-003-14873-9 (ebk)

DOI: 10.4324/9781003148739

Typeset in Sabon
by codeMantra

This book is lovingly dedicated to:

Leonore, who knew how to live for herself without being selfish and taught me several feisty Yiddish phrases. (L.B.F.)

Alvi, my beloved father, who truly embodied compassion and by example taught me to rely on my internal Finnish sisu. (C.K.)

Contents

List of Figures   xi
List of Tables   xiii
Preface   xv
Acknowledgments   xix

Part One: Two Cultures at Odds   1

1   The Situation: We Don't Understand Each Other   3

    Navigating Conflict   4
    Defining Concepts   6
    Intercultural Lenses   9
    Cultivating the Capacity to Understand the Perspective of the Other   10
    Reality Checks   12
    Charting a Path   14
    You Are Here   15
    Summary   16
    Practice and Reflection   16
    Resources   17
    References   17

2   Introduction to Each Culture: Administration and Faculty   20

    Tuning In   21
    Understanding Cultural Groups   22
    A Healthy Dose of Discourse   23
    The Administrator Perspective   28
    The Faculty Perspective   31
    Tricky, Sticky Transparency   34

CONTENTS

Weighing the Risks of Vulnerability 35
The Complex Notion of Power 35
What We Share and Agree Upon 36
Summary 37
Practice and Reflection 37
Resources 38
References 38

3 The Urgency: Higher Education Is Fighting for Survival   40

No Signal 41
Modality Matters 43
Faculty Perspectives 45
Administrator Perspectives 46
Accessibility Matters 47
Money Matters 50
Identity Matters 53
Re-envisioning the Landscape 57
Summary 57
Practice and Reflection 57
Resources 58
References 59

4 Why Us? An Administrator and Faculty Member Join Forces   61

Life in the Trenches 62
One Size Does not Fit All 63
Intercultural (R)evolution in Theory 66
Cultural Norms 67
Intercultural (R)evolution in Practice 68
The Journey Begins at Home 71
Preparing for the Journey 73
Summary 73
Practice and Reflection 74
Resources 74
References 75

Part Two: Two Cultures Building Bridges   77

5 Cultural Priority: Resources   79

Resources Under Threat 79
Faculty Member K's Perspective 83

Administrator S's Perspective   84
Cultural Context   85
Cultural Currency   88
Cultural Universals   90
Summary   91
Practice and Reflection   92
Resources   92
References   93

6 Cultural Priority: Territory   94

The Taxonomy of Territory   94
Administrator S's Perspective   98
Faculty Member K's Perspective   99
Territory in Context   100
The Boundary between Business and Academia   103
The Boundary between Academics and the College Experience   104
Building Trust Has Its Benefits   106
Summary   107
Practice and Reflection   107
Resources   108
References   109

7 Cultural Priority: Governance   110

Time and Tide Wait for No Institution   110
Faculty Member K's Perspective   115
Administrator S's Perspective   116
Governance in Context   117
Governance as Tug-of-War   120
Sharing Is Hard   122
Summary   124
Practice and Reflection   124
Resources   124
References   125

8 Cultural Priority: Tradition   127

The Science of Tradition   128
Administrator S's Perspective   131
Faculty Member K's Perspective   132
Tradition in Context   133
Immunity to Change   140

CONTENTS

Tradition and Identity 140
Traditions of Exclusion 142
Tradition and Transformation 144
Summary 144
Practice and Reflection 145
Resources 145
References 146

Part Three: Two Cultures, One Community   149

9 Cultural Imperative: Trust   151

In _____ We Trust 152
Faculty Member K's Perspective 157
Administrator S's Perspective 158
Trust in Context 158
Practice Listening 161
Practice Inclusive Leadership 163
Practice Compassion 165
Summary 166
Practice and Reflection 166
Resources 167
References 167

10 Beyond Theory: A Plan for Action   169

Environmental Toxins: Resilience and Risks 170
Practice Listening 172
Practice Inclusive Leadership 178
Practice Compassion 182
Conclusion 187
Summary 189
References 189

Index   191

Figures

1.1	Values that build trust	14
4.1	Cultivating the capacity to understand the perspective of the other	72
10.1	Cultural priorities and trust	173

Tables

3.1 Higher Education Headlines 41
4.1 Developing Global Fitness 69

Preface

For many decades, researchers motivated to examine the perennial conflicts between faculty and administrators in higher education have typically focused on external pressures and issues of accountability, or communication styles that can be changed to increase institutional efficiency. Nelson Rolihlahla Mandela (1919–2013), the antiapartheid activist who became South Africa's first Black head of state and the first democratically elected President, was acutely familiar with conflict throughout his lifetime. The conflicts that he experienced included dire situations and threatened fundamental human rights. Mandela described education as "the most powerful weapon which you can use to change the world." It is no accident that he chose the word "weapon," for the societal challenges that continue to engage global citizens often involve fighting of a literal nature. In a metaphorical sense, the fight for resources, territory, governance, and traditions is experienced on higher education campuses by community members who also believe, with all of their being, that education matters. Faculty and administrators in higher education dedicate their careers to working to achieve shared goals in this vein, with an internal compass that guides their values and beliefs.

At the time of this writing, the world has been focused on a common threat – the COVID-19 virus – that has challenged faculty and administrators to align their priorities and re-envision education in the midst of an uncertain, rapidly evolving pandemic. Scholars have recently turned their attention to examining higher education through a lens that highlights the uncertainty. For example, Blankenberger and Williams (2020) note that "[c]atastrophic events are change agents and when introduced into an ecological system, the system will react to achieve a new equilibrium" (p. 404). The field of education has reinvented itself many times in response to threats of a financial and/or political nature. The COVID-19 pandemic, however, generated ripples of disruption that called attention

PREFACE

to threats that are more extensive, raising questions and concerns about equity and access related to race and ethnicity and socioeconomic status, among other factors.

In their shared efforts to find the new equilibrium, it is not surprising that faculty and administrators have been deeply engaged in efforts that have reduced their perennial conflicts in some ways, and exacerbated them in other ways. *Building Trust Between Faculty and Administrators: An Intercultural Perspective* presents and critically examines faculty and administrators as members of higher education communities and as members of cultural groups that have different ways of experiencing their shared environment. Our work grew out of our own lived experiences as professionals in higher education and is anchored in the fundamental belief that "[f]inding points of understanding and mutual agreement is absolutely essential to overcoming the sometimes significant barrier standing between faculty and administration" (Koverola, 2016, para. 1).

We experience cultural differences every day – at times on a small yet meaningful scale, and sometimes in larger, more profound ways. Cultural differences are often obvious when we take the time to reflect and study them on an intellectual level. As we live our lives day to day, sometimes making decisions in the moment due to complicated factors, we are not evaluating every interaction we have on an intellectual level. It is frequently the case that we *feel* those interactions on an *emotional* level. In any given moment or during any disagreement, our instincts are often linked to survival and to staying loyal to what is familiar and valued.

This book is designed to integrate research with concrete examples drawn from actual experiences shared by faculty and administrators. We focus on intercultural communication, which we believe to be vital for institutions of higher education, as academic community members strive to cultivate the capacity to understand the perspective of the other. As active participants and learners, our respective communities "are places where culture is constantly renewed and reconstructed by those who participate in [and outside of] the classrooms" (Fiore, 2021, p. 3).

The case studies presented in this book were created as a result of real examples, experienced by faculty and administrators in institutions of higher education, that were communicated to the authors over years of research and professional interactions. To ensure confidentiality, names and details have been altered, and we have noted with humor and humility that many of the situations depicted in the case studies have been experienced by many different people working at many different institutions. These case studies are provided to engage readers in scenarios that present the perspective of a faculty member and/or administrator, and we have attempted to include a range of positions and occasions that will resonate with readers. Furthermore, we include questions at the end of each chapter, intended to prompt reflection and dialogue, as well as additional resources that can extend thinking and learning for individuals and communities.

Ultimately, we believe that thoughtful, though sometimes difficult, communication contributes to relationship "muscle" – what at first seems like a hard lift grows easier over time, with commitment to practice. As faculty and administrators develop a greater collective capacity for understanding the perspective of others in their academic communities, they are simultaneously investing in the health and wellbeing of their institutions and a more equitable and inclusive society.

REFERENCES

Blankenberger, B., & Williams, A.M. (2020). COVID and the impact on higher education: The essential role of integrity and accountability. *Administrative Theory & Praxis, 42*(3), pp. 404–423.

Fiore, L.B. (2021). *Assessment of young children: A collaborative approach* (2nd ed.). Routledge.

Koverola, C. (2016, January 27). Bridging the gap between administrators and faculty with an intercultural perspective. *The Evolllution: A Modern Campus Illumination*. Retrieved at https://evolllution.com/managing-institution/operations_efficiency/bridging-the-gap-between-administrators-and-faculty-with-an-intercultural-perspective/

Acknowledgments

This book has grown out of many years of experiences and research in higher education. We are extremely grateful for the support and inspiration that contributed to the evolution of our work and to the opportunities that presented themselves throughout our careers – some of which felt extremely difficult to endure, yet wound up teaching us the most.

As our research progressed from the kernel of an idea through waves of data collection and analysis, conversations with numerous friends, colleagues, and mentors played a significant role in re-focusing or challenging us, and the work is stronger as a result of the process. In particular, we are grateful to those who continue to reflect on their own practices, and to un-learn practices that have existed for centuries and have recently been challenged by those willing to take risks in the interest of equity and inclusion. We are inspired by students who have contributed to research efforts, such as Kiara Maher, Kiera Rowe, Yirui Su, and Michael Wessel. We are grateful to Kim Perez who joined us in endless hours of conversation, laughter, and tears as we analyzed our data, reviewed our findings, and ultimately birthed this manuscript.

And our respective families:

To Talia, Matthew, and Steve – for listening and validating in the midst of many puzzles, for offering playlist suggestions, and for knowing when it was time to pick up take-out. (L.B.F.)

To Natasha – you are my inspiration to always forge ahead – and to Ian, for your nurturance and unwavering support in always helping me maintain perspective. I couldn't have done it without you both! (C.K.)

Part One

Two Cultures at Odds

Chapter One

The Situation: We Don't Understand Each Other

"*Huh?*"

For years, we used this one word as the working title for this book. One reason for this is that the simple question reveals a significant dissatisfaction among faculty members and administrators working in institutions of higher education. The other reason is that the playful working title mitigated many tensions that emerged as we grappled with scenarios throughout years of research and professional experience as – and with – faculty and administrators. These two groups are so often at odds, it's almost as if they represent different cultures that have no method of effective communication. Rampant conflict and misunderstandings impede much-needed institutional change, adversely affect students' experiences, and threaten the very viability of many institutions that are already under scrutiny due to myriad factors (Horn, 2018; Whitford, 2021; Zahneis, 2021). While the topic of interpersonal dynamics is validated in numerous research articles that may be read by members of their respective professional organizations, such work tends to focus on discrete "problems," such as budget, governance, and enrollment challenges (e.g., Kiley, 2013; Shinn, 2014), rather than collaboration and the hard work of sustaining authentic relationships that make navigating such problems more successful, in spite of outcomes that appease constituents.

This book takes the unusual approach of acknowledging multiple perspectives and intentionally articulating and using them to advance mutual goals. While writing this book, we recognized that in our respective roles of professor and university president, we thereby simultaneously serve as guides on a journey, cultural ambassadors and/or brokers, and participant researchers inviting readers to consider complicated professional cultures, offer translations, and share common frustrations and confusions about the other.

Why? Because institutions of higher education were struggling financially and in the public perception before the COVID-19 crisis exacerbated perennial tensions (e.g., Ehrenberg, 2012; Shinn, 2014). If faculty members and administrators remain entrenched at an impasse rather than team up to harness their collective resources and build a thriving future together, their institutions and employment will suffer. The stakes are high. People are tired of feeling misunderstood, tired of being accused of nefarious intent, tired of not being trusted. But people are also tired of being so suspicious, and yearn for trusting relationships that allow them to relax and focus on their work (Hoppes & Holley, 2014). The lack of understanding is exhausting, and impedes a shared mission: to provide high-quality education that contributes to a compassionate and productive society.

NAVIGATING CONFLICT

Conflict between higher education faculty and administrators is not a new phenomenon, but it is deeply unfortunate. All too often, such conflict and misunderstanding impedes innovation and institutional change that will significantly benefit students and society. While the value of establishing mutual understanding between these two key constituent groups is self-evident, a sustainable practice of listening without judgment as a component of broader understanding and institutional change remains perplexingly elusive.

To illustrate clear differences in perceptions and interpretations, what follows below are snippets from focus group conversations held among faculty members and administrators, respectively, following a simulated academic meeting. An announcement had been made that a program was going to be terminated and "taught out" for students currently in the pipeline.

Faculty members' comments included:

- "You'd think they would work with us to try to improve the program, to build up numbers."
- "They just thought, 'Here's a way to save some money and let's go on.'"
- "This is a college, a university – there's a reason for these four years. How do you decide to cut a core component of a liberal arts education? That doesn't make any sense to me."
- "My concern is [cutting a program] makes it look [to the board] like you're doing something. Instead of actually accomplishing anything, it's making it look like we're being proactive, whether it solves it or not."
- "[T]he communication isn't there. So, we come to the conversation with suspicion, and it doesn't always feel like it's above-board shared decision-making, like we've been asking for."

- "I feel like faculty look at it from a curriculum-based, long-term perspective – what's good for the school ten years from now – and that administration is constantly trying to put band-aids on gashes and do immediate change to cover up that hole. 'Let's cover up that hole, let's cover up that hole.'"

Administrators' comments included:

- "We've been trying for a year to talk about this. I thought we included faculty [in those discussions]. We had meetings, they were welcome, they were invited, but they didn't always show up. But we would post the minutes. It's not like this was some secret thing, but that's how they acted, like I had pulled something on them and blindsided them. They were shocked and critical."
- "I'm actually puzzled. I mean I could've sent more emails reminding them that this was going to happen, but then it sounds kind of threatening. It's almost like after a communication went out, it fell into a hole – like they never processed it."
- "They would've been happy to keep on talking for another year, but I got the feeling that they weren't getting that there's dollars and cents attached to it; there's a monetary factor. It's like the business end of education – the fiscal end of education – it's like they don't believe it."
- "Historically, [this program niche] is important knowledge, but can we as a school afford to have such a specialized course that has six or eight students? We can't afford it."
- "There's no recognition that it was a difficult decision that somebody had to make. It would be nice, once in a while, to get someone to say, 'I know that was really hard, and I don't agree with you, but I know it was hard.'"
- "I get the feeling they'd be completely happy talking about this for years, and acting as if there's no monetary hit. It's almost like I betrayed them by making a decision. But that's growing up, right? There comes a time when you have to make a decision."

When we consider two disparate groups, they may have significant differences in their values, beliefs, customs, language, and communication patterns, to name a few. The result of these differences and a lack of understanding can lead to a process of "othering," where one group views the "other" as different, perhaps as threatening and dangerous, or simply as bad. The other is rarely viewed as good or as a group that one should approach. The human tendency with othering is to demonize and cast aspersions, thereby securing the safety and security of one's own comfortable, familiar group.

In fact, those who venture into a space of dialogue with the other can be viewed as traitors by members of their respective group. We have seen faculty be accused by other faculty members of "kissing-up" when they engage in honest dialogue with administrators in an effort to build bridges. Similarly, administrators who manage to develop strong relationships with faculty are often cast by their administrative colleagues as "too faculty-friendly."

Framing these differences between faculty and administrators as *cultural* differences provides a neutral scaffolding from which to facilitate discussion and develop shared understanding. Further, an examination of perceived or actual cultural differences inevitably elucidates areas of common values and beliefs. We have come to learn that differences will often reveal themselves in the interpretation and living out of these values, which are essentially cultural customs, language, and communication patterns.

DEFINING CONCEPTS

So we pose the question: is an intercultural perspective useful in building trust between faculty and administrators in higher education? In order to begin to investigate this question, we must first establish definitions of key terms that appear throughout this book.

Culture

The term "culture" is one that can be used in many ways, for many purposes, across academic disciplines and common parlance at any given time. Depending on the moment and the intention, people consider culture to be:

> ...something that people live inside of like a country or a region or a building – they speak, for example, of people leaving their cultures and going to live in other people's cultures. Some consider culture something people think, a set of beliefs or values or mental patterns that people in a particular group share. Still others regard culture more like a set of rules that people follow...and others think of it as a set of largely unconscious habits that govern people's behavior without them fully realizing it.
> (Scollon, Scollon, & Jones, 2012, p. 3)

We recognize the potentially confusing lived experience of being part of a culture that is defined from within and from without, and perhaps differently by individuals based on their own personal and professional being. We are therefore grateful to the field of academia, broadly, for providing a culture in which "culture" may be explored through different lenses. We are grateful to Scollon, Scollon, and Jones (2012), specifically, for their definition of culture that captures the spirit of this book: culture is "a way of dividing people up into groups according to some feature of these people which helps us to understand something about them and how they are different from or similar to other people" (p. 3).

Cross-cultural

Simply put, "cross-cultural" refers to a comparison between two or more cultures. Though admittedly simplistic, in order to understand cross-cultural approaches to research, scholars posit that context is important, since "one query may present different findings in different places" (Akpovo, Moran, & Brookshire, 2018, p. xxi). Thus, comparison provides an opportunity for researchers to examine differences and similarities that exist between or among groups. Since collaborative cross-cultural research invites negotiation and co-construction of understanding, experts in the field of cross-cultural research acknowledge that there is sometimes a "blurring of the lines" between cross-cultural and intercultural relationships (Liamputtong, 2010). Researchers who engage in cross-cultural studies often find themselves challenged, and ultimately transformed, as a result of culturally sensitive practice.

Intercultural

As noted above, "intercultural" implies a relationship in which the research process transforms the knowledge and behaviors of participants by virtue of the exchanges, investigations, and connections formed. People "are prompted to scrutinize the different underlying assumptions and schemas in both cultures" (Lu et al., 2017, p. 1093). Whereas cross-cultural research investigates cultural systems as discrete entities, intercultural research explores "'people doing things' using systems of culture" (Scollon, Scollon, & Jones, 2012, p. 5). Researchers have noted that it is a mistake to focus research on culture as a key to "understanding" when many "misunderstandings" are actually "linguistic" in nature or "based on inequality" and therefore reflect "global inequality and injustice" that can be obscured in pursuit of cultural understanding (Piller, 2012, p. 9).

The focus of intercultural communication "must shift from reified and inescapable notions of cultural difference to...discourses where 'culture' is actually made relevant and used as a communicative resource" (p. 14).

Diversity

As a term, "diversity" can be used to encompass everything and therefore nothing. "Without a precise definition of categories...diversity as such is absolutely meaningless and risks being used for the purpose of everybody undermining any idea of equity" (Klein, 2016, p. 151). In our research into faculty and administrator relationships and experiences, it is precisely because we cannot (and do not seek to) isolate inextricably linked identities and experiences that comprise an individual's understanding and participation within a group that we choose an intercultural lens with which to examine faculty and administrator relationships. "Race, ethnicity, social class, language use, gender, sexual orientation, religion, ability, and other social and human differences" (Nieto & Bode, 2018, p. 4) contribute to the range of diversity evident in institutions of higher education. It is critically important to acknowledge that diversity and diversity in high education settings are nestled in a socio-political context that has influenced the writing of this book. While not necessarily at the forefront of every chapter, we have attempted to be cognizant of diversity in its broadest, complicated sense as we present and process the case studies, anecdotes, and research woven throughout this book.

Communication

Communication is one of many tools used by members of a cultural group to convey ideas to others (Scollon, Scollon, & Jones, 2012). This can include language, as well as other tools that transmit information, such as physical and digital technologies, manners and social conventions, and images and ideologies.

Governance

Colleges and universities typically operate with unique decision-making strategies and systems that evolve over time. In 1966, the American Association of University Professors (AAUP) published a statement suggesting a "shared" governance model, describing "shared responsibility and cooperative action among the components of the academic institution. The statement [was] intended to foster constructive joint thought and action, both within the institutional structure and in protection of its integrity against improper intrusions" (AAUP, 2020). Furthermore, the statement acknowledges variation among institutions and offers hope that the statement and "the principles asserted will lead to the correction of existing weaknesses and assist in the establishment of sound structures and procedures" (AAUP, 2020) including: academic freedom, budget and planning, financial exigency, and the hiring and evaluation of faculty and administrators.

INTERCULTURAL LENSES

Now revisit the comments made by faculty and administrators with regard to the hypothetical "teaching-out" of a program, presented earlier. Elements related to all of the terms in the previous section may be highlighted for a closer examination at the cultural landscape of higher education. However, an intercultural lens allows us to look at the cultural systems of both faculty and administrators with respect to the viability of an academic program. Consider the following analysis of values and beliefs inherent in faculty and administrator cultural systems, posited by Koverola (2016), which may inform your own self-reflection and analysis of your institutional setting:

Values Embedded in Programs

- **Faculty**: Programs must align with the institutional mission, be academically rigorous, and serve students well.
- **Administrator**: Programs must align with the institutional mission, adhere to relevant external professional/disciplinary standards, provide evidence of academic outcomes that serve students well, and be financially viable.

Beliefs about Programs

- **Faculty**: Programs that have essential historical value to the institution deserve additional resources to make them feasible and sustainable. Programs that are sufficiently resourced will continue to thrive and remain inherently valuable; there will rarely be a need to cancel certain programs.
- **Administrator**: The current need for programs is impacted by the related forces in a competitive market. Limited institutional resources need to be allocated based on current enrollments and future projections. Programs that are not financially viable according to market analysis and revenue/expense ratios must be carefully examined, modified to become financially stable, or terminated.

A quick look at both the differences and similarities reveals where there is common ground between these two cultural groups. It also reveals how an action plan emanating from the respective values and beliefs could differ for the two groups. A potentially productive intercultural approach would include discourse: about how proposed and/or desired outcomes will vary depending upon the values and beliefs of the constituent groups. Neither group is right or wrong, good or bad – the groups are simply different and guided by their respective cultures. In order to attain institutional endurance with perspective-taking, institutional citizens must practice and prepare for intercultural discourse.

CULTIVATING THE CAPACITY TO UNDERSTAND THE PERSPECTIVE OF THE OTHER

Think about how you prepare to travel to another country. You may plan your itinerary by browsing guidebooks and websites to learn about that country's sights, events, and attractions. You will likely try to learn some key phrases in an unfamiliar language so you will be able to communicate with the local community members while you're there. You might even investigate the cuisine before you go, engaging multiple senses as you start to get excited about experiencing customs and practices different from your own.

In other words, you are actively seeking out new knowledge and trying to understand a culture that's different from yours. You are anticipating differences and similarities, and you are looking for ways to bridge some gaps so that you can connect with people as much as possible.

Admittedly, voluntary travel is unique because you are *choosing* to have a cross-cultural experience, and that experience is automatically framed as a joyful experience. Any communication difficulties you encounter will be added to your favorite party anecdote repertoire. Even if you encounter bigger challenges, like transportation mishaps or lost luggage, if those challenges happen within a context of vacation they often can be accepted with good humor. However, when we encounter similar cultural divides in our everyday work lives – while trying to meet deadlines, teach students, conduct research, run a university – we don't tend to view these as potential party anecdotes. More often, they become fodder for collegial venting.

In fact, at virtually any faculty meeting you will hear faculty protest over the latest administrative edict and incursion upon what is deemed academic purview:

"Administrators just don't understand the slippery slope of their decisions."
"They are watering down academic rigor."
"They are interfering with best practices/pedagogy by increasing class caps."
"They are violating our academic freedom."

"They are pressuring us to increase online offerings when it's never as good as face-to-face."

Similarly, at any gathering of higher education administrators, the conversation inevitably turns to the topic of faculty. You hear comments on the faculty's lack of appreciation of institutional financial pressures ("Can't you just increase class size?"), or the need to be nimble ("Two years of planning doesn't constitute nimble!"), or how online teaching really can be effective ("There's no turning back post-COVID!"), or how not being in compliance with deadlines really does have consequences ("Faculty, please submit your grades on time."). The list goes on and on.

Knowing the Players

For anyone seeking comic relief about this perennially tense state of affairs, a favorite parody on the topic is the novel *Straight Man* by Richard Russo (1997). The setting is a nondescript unionized mid-size public institution, and the characters and the dynamics they play out are familiar in virtually every higher education institution in North America. The characters may have different names than the ones at your present institution, but you will recognize them all and undoubtedly recognize yourself as well. What follows are some common archetypes that tend to have negative associations for members of the "other" group.

Faculty Archetypes

- The *prima donna*: Faculty who are brilliant and renowned in their specialized fields, but feet never touch the ground.
- The *workhorse*: Faculty who volunteer for every committee and go above and beyond typical responsibilities, thereby creating expectations for above-average participation.
- The *"should-be-retired"*: Faculty who aren't quite keeping up with current teaching methods or technology and/or who complain loudly and often yet offer no solutions.
- The *token*: Faculty who are of under-represented groups and are asked to represent these group(s) on numerous committees, ultimately resulting in work imbalances and burnout.

Administrator Archetypes

- The *former faculty*: Administrators who came up through the ranks – either earned or due to relationships with those in power – and feel a certain superiority to those below.

- The *outsiders*: Administrators whose prior careers fell outside of academia (often business-related), who feel the mistrust or resentment from the "insiders."
- The *short-timers*: Administrators who move around from institution to institution, often with a multi-step ladder in mind that leads to their "dream" job.
- The *narcissists*: No further explanation needed.

In both faculty and administrator cultures, there are additional predictable sub-groups. Seeing your world laid out in cringe-worthy humorous detail in a novel can be cathartic, as we see that we're not alone in our experiences and in our frustrations.

REALITY CHECKS

As authors of this book, we will either speak as "we" or refer to ourselves specifically to provide clarification as a faculty or administrator regarding an issue that we have experienced personally. Over the course of our professional and personal relationship, spanning more than a decade, we have shared our own stories and frustrations with each other often. It's common for us to call each other just to investigate something that seems "off" or dig deeper into something that we don't understand through our one-way lens. *Why would a faculty member say that? Why would an administrator act that way? What is going on?* But before writing this book, our first step was to examine our own perspectives: do others have these same frustrating experiences with the other as we do? Do others have the same confusion about the other as we do? We sought outside perspectives by getting input from others.

Collaborative Research

To explore these themes, we embarked on a mixed methods study, engaging faculty and administrator participants in higher education settings. Most participants worked and resided in the United States, though we did reach out to colleagues in Canada and Israel in later stages of our research. The first phase of our research involved surveys sent to faculty and administrators utilizing an anonymous online platform. Phase two included focus groups to examine some emerging themes that we identified in the survey responses. The first focus groups took place in person and consisted of all faculty and all administrator participants, respectively. We also conducted one focus group that combined faculty and administrators together (anonymously, with images and identities hidden) utilizing an online meeting platform. We have also conducted countless individual conversations with faculty members and administrators over many years and maintained ongoing records of our own observations and experiences within higher education. Our research has also included thorough review of the relevant literature, stemming from curiosity as well as commitment to learning that informs our own practice.

We immediately discovered overwhelming agreement that faculty–administrator relationships are fraught. Some faculty participants described their work cultures using words like "fear and despair," "embattled," "poisoning," "under attack," "hostile," and "adversarial." On a very different note, other respondents called their cultures "collegial," "cordial," "collaborative," "supportive," and "friendly." In our survey, just one faculty member out of the 43 who responded to a question about their biggest frustrations with administrators reported no frustration. Other questions yielded answers that revealed tensions ranging from not feeling heard and not being consulted regarding decisions that affect them, to a sense of administrators being out of touch with the needs of faculty and administrators having lost sight of the purpose of higher education.

Administrators' responses provide evidence that many are familiar with – and resent – the accusations that they are losing sight of education's purpose. Their most-cited frustration is that, in their perspective, faculty don't know the business of education and don't consider the big picture. As a result, misunderstandings about resource allocation and conflicts about governance were second and third on their list of grievances. Overall, they had a more positive view of the institutions' work cultures, describing them as "collaborative" and "collegial." Of course, as administrators they likely have more influence (or at least perceived influence) over those work cultures. They also perceive that they have a greater "stake" in having their cultures described in positive terms as they are essentially held responsible for the institutional culture. In subsequent chapters, we'll address how power plays a role in these faculty–administrator relationships.

We also discovered that faculty and administrators are tired of the tensions. They articulate a desire for a work environment anchored in trust, and as a result of numerous conversations, we came to wonder if people *do* want to build trust, or do they simply want their workplaces to be different, and better? We propose that a community guided by trust is indeed better, and attainable. But trust isn't simply a matter of will. It's often the result of a deliberate strategy for understanding the perspectives or goals of another. With our compass pointing toward trust, this book will combine our expertise in the field of higher education with an intercultural communication approach to provide you with practical tools that support the development and implementation of trust-building strategies in your own professional community.

TWO CULTURES AT ODDS

CHARTING A PATH

We lay out a roadmap by presenting faculty and administrators as two different cultures whose members will likely work together more harmoniously and productively if they understand each other's perspective, values, and beliefs. We address these themes from our own unique perspectives as:

- representatives of our respective cultural groups, having the hard conversations and negotiating the complexities of these relationships every day
- experts in intercultural communication and education
- women

It is important to also acknowledge the limits of our own perspectives, and the perspectives that we do not have. For these reasons, we are committed to our own continuous learning (and un-learning), which involves reckoning with how we have benefitted from structures in higher education that maintain inequitable, discriminatory practices. This stance undergirds our belief that trust exists when members of all groups feel (or experience) a sense of being valued, seen, heard, and respected. Figure 1.1 illustrates this phenomenon.

In the chapters that follow, we will examine how our cultural identities as faculty and as administrators shape and are shaped by each of those areas. As mentioned earlier in this chapter, perceived cultural disagreements are often rooted in a misunderstanding – one that has interrupted one

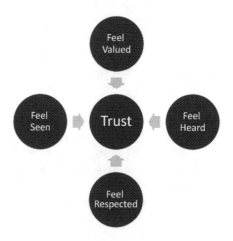

Figure 1.1 Values that build trust.

or more of these essential elements. We feel unseen, or we are not seeing someone else. We feel unheard, or we are not hearing someone else. As a result, trust is violated. In order to repair it, we must cultivate the capacity to understand the perspective of the other.

The chapters that follow explore what it looks like to put intercultural communication skills to use, addressing some common themes that create and sustain tension by analyzing both sides of actual scenarios that will be readily familiar to anyone working in a college or university setting. These topics have been addressed in related literature, but the research tends to stop short of identifying solutions and instead focus on how different "sides" in higher education become entrenched in their values and ideologies (e.g., Harris & Hartley, 2011; Kezar & Eckel, 2002).

Together, we move beyond theory. We aim to provide a cultural analogy that you can use (on your own or with peers) to identify your *guide*, learn the *language*, understand the cultural *currency*, and more – to cultivate capacity to understand the perspective of the other and build trust across and within an academic community. Every chapter in Part Two is anchored in theory *and* application, and case studies illustrate real experiences for faculty, administrators, and other higher education community members. This framework establishes a focus on workplace relationships viewed through an intercultural lens, promoting critical thinking and moving beyond catchphrases and current jargon to invaluable application and trust-building. In Part Three, we provide resources and activities that faculty members and administrators may use in higher education settings. The activities have been designed and tested by employees in institutions of higher education across the country and abroad. Discussion questions at the end of every chapter provide entry points for you to discuss chapter material with members of your own educational group culture and across groups, as you gain familiarity with content and build "muscle" and confidence to recognize and anticipate alternative perspectives. Additional online resources provided at the end of each chapter bridge research and practice, promoting an active rather than passive stance in the interest of strengthening relationships in and out of the higher education setting.

YOU ARE HERE

If you don't currently experience the tensions described in this book, then you are fortunate (or have yet to acknowledge them), and as a beloved mentor of one of the authors used to muse, "Denial is a most comfortable state in which to reside." The inspiration for writing this book was not to convince others of the challenges they do not realize that they are experiencing. Some people experience tensions and see no value in trying to understand them or eliminate them. Others would rather avoid the discomfort that accompanies disequilibrium – understanding a new or different perspective sometimes rattles foundations and produces more questions than answers. The motivation for writing this book grew out of experiences that will resonate with the many well-meaning faculty members and administrators who are genuinely mystified by the "other." In the words of one administrator cited earlier, "I'm actually puzzled." In our combined 50+ years of experience in higher education, we have encountered and spoken with many people who are simply puzzled. This book provides concrete tools and strategies to help you gain an understanding of differing perspectives in higher education settings, and how to move beyond understanding toward positive action. In Chapter Two, we present faculty and administrator cultures – examining characteristics, vulnerabilities, and boundaries – as we imagine a firm foundation of trust.

SUMMARY

Faculty and administrators in higher education settings predictably complain about the other, and express dissatisfaction with the other, without necessarily understanding the group culture in which the others reside. Using an intercultural approach, common conflicts between faculty and administrators may be viewed as socially co-constructed conflicts related to power as opposed to simply "misunderstandings" related to a lack of understanding about language or customs. As we cultivate a capacity for understanding the perspectives of faculty members and administrators, we are building a foundation of trust – one that can withstand both familiar and unprecedented challenges.

PRACTICE AND REFLECTION

1. Several issues were presented that weave through higher education settings, such as economics, politics, and societal expectations. Why do you think these are perennial issues? Examine each one individually and articulate reasons for the timeless influence of these factors.
2. Throughout the chapter, the important role of communication was stressed. What are some ways that you communicate? How do you prefer to receive communication? Think about your own habits and comfort levels, and cite some ways these have influenced your expectations for communication in your work environment.
3. Consider the need for accountability in higher education contexts. How do you weigh the need against the value that it has in your

everyday work life? Think of an example from your own experience and describe how the assessment process included others (faculty, administrators, staff), accordingly.

RESOURCES

Cultural Humility

https://www.youtube.com/watch?v=c_wOnJJEfxE

This brief YouTube video provides a distinction between the terms "cultural competence" and "cultural humility," with the latter being a more advanced way of being and interacting with others. Whereas competence implies knowledge, humility implies a stance that includes reflection and awareness of one's own biases that influence interactions with others.

An Introduction to Ethnography

https://www.scribbr.com/methodology/ethnography/

This website provides an overview of the research method known as ethnography. A qualitative research method, ethnography provides flexibility that is valued by many researchers and scholar-practitioners. This method also affords an opportunity for reflection and consideration of one's relationship to the group, ethical principles, and how one can remain mindful of biases and assumptions that influence perception and interpretation.

Some Challenges Being a Cultural Ambassador

https://www.newyorker.com/culture/cultural-comment/the-difficulty-of-being-a-cultural-ambassador-for-america

This article serves as a mirror that reflects current challenges and tensions that underlie the writing of this book at the present time. The author notes her hope for a shared goal with the audience she describes in the piece: "…to better understand phenomena that were rapidly affecting us all." This goal remains at the core of the writing of this book, which will move us toward action that reduces tensions and increases collaboration in higher education contexts.

REFERENCES

American Association of University Professors. (2020). *Shared governance*. Retrieved at https://www.aaup.org/our-programs/shared-governance

Akpovo, S.M., Moran, M.J., & Brookshire, R. (2018). *Collaborative cross-cultural research methodologies in early care and education contexts*. Routledge.

Ehrenberg, R.G. (2012). American higher education in transition. *Journal of Economic Perspectives, 26*(1), pp. 193–216.

Harris, M.S., & Hartley, M. (2011, November/December). Witch-Hunting at Crucible University: The power and peril of competing organizational ideologies. *The Journal of Higher Education, 82*(6), pp. 691–719.

Hoppes, C.R., & Holley, K.A. (2014). Organizational trust in times of challenge: The impact on faculty and administrators. *Innovative Higher Education, 39*(3), pp. 201–216.

Horn, M.B. (2018). Will half of all colleges really close in the next decade? *Forbes*. Retrieved at https://www.forbes.com/sites/michaelhorn/2018/12/13/will-half-of-all-colleges-really-close-in-the-next-decade/?sh=5b263ec252e5

Kezar, A.J., & Eckel, P. (2002). The effect of institutional culture on change strategies in higher education: Universal principles or culturally responsive concepts? *The Journal of Higher Education, 73*, pp. 435–460.

Kiley, K. (2013, January 17). Nowhere to turn. *Inside Higher Ed*. Retrieved at https://www.insidehighered.com/news/2013/01/17/moodys-report-calls-question-all-traditional-university-revenue-sources

Klein, U. (2016). Gender equality and diversity politics in higher education: Conflicts, challenges, and requirements for collaboration. *Women's Studies International Forum, 54*, pp. 147–156.

Koverola, C. (2016, January 27). Bridging the gap between administrators and faculty with an intercultural perspective. *The Evolllution: A Modern Campus Illumination*. Retrieved at https://evolllution.com/-managing-institution/operations_efficiency/bridging-the-gap-between-administrators-and-faculty-with-an-intercultural-perspective/

Liamputtong, P. (2010). *Performing qualitative cross-cultural research*. Cambridge University Press.

Lu, J.G., Hafenbrack, A.C., Eastwick, P.W., Wang, D.J., Maddux, W.W., & Galinsky, A.D. (2017). "Going out" of the box: Close intercultural friendships and romantic relationships spark creativity, workplace innovation, and entrepreneurship. *Journal of Applied Psychology, 102*(7), pp. 1091–1108.

Nieto, S., & Bode, P. (2018). *Affirming diversity: The sociopolitical context of multicultural education* (7th ed.). Pearson.

Piller, I. (2012). Intercultural communication: An overview. In C.B. Paulston, S.F. Kiesling, & E.S. Rangel (Eds.), *The handbook of intercultural discourse and communication*. John Wiley & Sons.

Scollon, R., Scollon, S.W., & Jones, R.H. (2012). *Intercultural communication: A discourse approach*. Wiley-Blackwell.

Shinn, L.D. (2014, August 8). Top down or bottom up? Leadership and shared governance on campus. *Change: The Magazine of Higher Learning*, 46(4), pp. 52–55.

Whitford, E. (2021, May 6). No-confidence vote at Mills amid closure plans. *Inside Higher Ed*. Retrieved at https://www.insidehighered.com/quicktakes/2021/05/06/no-confidence-vote-mills-amid-closure-plans

Zahneis, M. (2021, May 7). A historic decline in U.S. births signals more enrollment troubles. *The Chronicle of Higher Education*. Retrieved at https://www.chronicle.com/article/a-historic-decline-in-u-s-births-signals-more-enrollment-troubles?cid=gen_sign_in

Chapter Two

Introduction to Each Culture: Administration and Faculty

"People have no idea the *hell* I'm in every moment!"

That's a direct quote from a participant in the research study that grounded our current understandings and prompted further investigation in higher education settings. Who do you think proclaimed the above statement?

1. An administrator
2. A faculty member

It doesn't matter who said it, because the proclaimer was anonymous and the fact is that it is something that could be uttered by someone in either role at any point on any day throughout their careers. While someone actually did make the statement above with requisite emphasis and dramatic flair, we are not able to discern or disclose their specific role. As real – and painfully humorous by association – as that quote might be, administrators and faculty members often experience challenges in their academic settings that cause genuinely stressful and unpleasant emotional and physical consequences. If "[c]ulture is the glue that binds organizations together" (Rosowsky & Hallman, 2020), then it is critically important for institutions of higher education to understand cultural perspectives in an academic setting. This goal is inherently difficult because higher education is already territory that is hard to define, due to political, social, economic, and other factors that are interrelated and, at times, more or less prevalent as climate trends shift over time.

Rosowsky and Hallman challenge academic citizens and stakeholders to examine culture further with provocative questions:

> Is culture universal, or ubiquitous, throughout the institution? Is it baked into the college itself, or espoused only by the president? And how does an institution articulate values that often go unspoken or

DOI: 10.4324/9781003148739-3

have never been formally asserted or documented? Do those values translate outside the college? Do they have relevance? Do they inspire the same emotions and commitments they do within the college community? Do they resonate? How can culture be widely adopted, promoted and celebrated? If clued into correctly, the 'who' is constant – even amid leadership changes, as new classes of students rotate in and out.

(Rosowsky & Hallman, 2020, par. 8–9)

TUNING IN

The following statements articulate some compelling thoughts shared in a focus group discussion that included administrators and faculty members from different academic institutions. See what you notice and/or identify about the speaker's words as you consider their statements. How does this noticing influence your perspective about the respective cultural group to which the speaker belongs? When we start making room for authentic, judgment-free conversations, we can learn a lot about others, as well as our own assumptions.

Faculty member:

> One thing I've been struggling with recently is feeling like some of the administrators who never held faculty positions don't understand the job. So, when we have moments of crisis, I don't know that they have the knowledge to make decisions that are always best for faculty and students. Our interests may be at odds. It's easy for me to feel like we're the heart and soul of this place with students. So, to make decisions that disrespect that workflow and that relationship we have with students can feel hurtful. When administrators don't have faculty experience, it's hard for me to trust those decisions.

Administrator, in direct response to the previous comment:

> I don't come from a faculty background. I have immense respect for faculty. It's disappointing to know that simply because I haven't come from that same background that there's an automatic assumption of a lack of empathy or lack of understanding. I mean, it makes sense. But I wish our faculty could know just how much time and thought go into the decisions that do get made, and the conversations that are had about, 'How does this impact faculty and how does it impact their ability to teach?' Especially with COVID, there

wasn't time for much shared governance in the beginning. It was a hot bomb dropped in the middle. I spent hours in classrooms in order to understand what the challenges were, what the technology was doing for them or not, how the students were interacting or not—in order to better understand what they're going through. I would appreciate the assumption of positive intent before the assumption of being capricious with decision-making.

As mentioned in the previous chapter, frustrations attributed to cultural misunderstandings may actually be related to an absence of discourse with others who are part of a culture or group different from the one we imagine for ourselves (Piller, 2012). So, one of the first steps we can take is to get to know each other individually and also make an effort to learn about each other's culture and perspective.

UNDERSTANDING CULTURAL GROUPS

As authors of this book, we currently represent an administrator and a faculty member perspective (different groups) and work at different institutions of higher education (different groups), and we met while serving as deans (same group) at the same institution (same group). We are both White women (same group), wives (same group), and mothers (same group), and we observe different religious traditions (different group). We live in different states (different group), though we have both lived in the same western state (same group), and we both enjoy cappuccinos (same group) and have pet dogs (same group). We therefore recognize that we can draw lines around us that embrace us in our similarity at the very same time that there are some enclosures within which we do not situate ourselves together. As with all social groups, some groups consist of people who are "meaningfully related to each other" and others consist of people who happen to be "in the same place at the same time but who are not connected" (Jhangiani & Tarry, 2019, par. 1). This inclination toward recognizing a group as a group has been characterized in social psychology literature as "entitativity...*the perception, either by the group members themselves or by others, that the people together are a group*" (par. 2). It is in this way that we imagine and define our own group cultures, including the broad academic culture in which we have worked for many decades. Therefore, as members of academic culture, we – along with many readers of this book – have been in countless meetings, listening to members of a specific faculty or administrative group, finding ourselves thinking, "Are you kidding me?" or "Right on!" These reactions are typically evoked in academic social gatherings, as well as in conversations where we are attempting (pretending?) to listen while we are actually evaluating the "other" and plotting our counter-moves in our head.

Over the course of our professional and personal relationship, we've also been in many conversations asking each other, "So, why did you make that decision? I don't agree with it, but help me understand. Here's my perspective." We have established trust that assures us that the other will be honest and open-minded.

A HEALTHY DOSE OF DISCOURSE

We are firmly convinced that administrators and faculty members can experience this type of trust and honest communication if the members of academic institutions commit to work together to develop a greater capacity for listening and understanding different perspectives. We therefore acknowledge that we are in a unique position to combine our professional understanding of intercultural communications, our personal experiences working with each other, and integrate the findings of our research with others who are also members of these cultural groups in academia. To begin, we offer definitions for some of the terms and roles that are used to identify people within the cultures we are examining (particularly in the United States) and therefore provide vocabulary that can inform future communication.

Administration

As previously noted, it is common for some administrators to have worked their way "through the ranks" or "up the ladder" in order to attain their current positions. In some institutions, administrators are required to teach at least one class during the academic year so that they retain connections to students and their fields of study. In most institutions, however, administrators do not teach classes or interact with students on a regular basis. It is often when problems arise that administrators are in contact with students, or when annual celebratory events are held at various points during an academic term, year, or cycle. Many administrators seek their positions because they truly believe that they can utilize their knowledge and skills to influence an academic environment for the common good. The following terms relate to the culture of administration.

President

The president of a college or university is considered the Chief Executive Officer (CEO) of the institution or, in some cases, a system of institutions.

The president is responsible to many constituent groups, including a governing board that typically hires and evaluates the president over the course of a contract period. The president provides leadership and vision for the short- and long-term planning and operations, as well as any strategic planning and implementation efforts. While a president may or may not interact directly with every constituent group connected with an institution, they are accountable to every group, including students and alumni, families, employees, donors, community members, and the field of higher education. This means that a strong and competent president will work to understand every aspect of the institution's existence – from tuition to cafeteria food, and from diversity, equity, inclusion, and justice (DEIJ) initiatives to classroom technology.

Chancellor

Often used synonymously with the title of president, a chancellor may be the executive leader of one university campus or the executive leader of the system as a whole. For example, the Colorado University (CU) system has the president as the executive head, and the State University of New York (SUNY) system has the chancellor as the head of its system. As confusing as this may be, a chancellor that is the CEO for an institution (or system) is responsible for all academic, financial, and general administrative matters (e.g., communications, emergencies, facilities, fundraising).

Provost

A provost is typically second in the hierarchy of executive positions in higher education, reporting to the president (or chancellor) in terms of setting and attaining goals for institutions. The primary role of the provost is to serve as the Chief Academic Officer (CAO). At some institutions, this role is referred to as Vice President for Academic Affairs, depending on institutional practices and/or the preference of the president. The provost's work is primarily internally focused on academics, and the hiring and retention of faculty, in contrast to other members of the senior leadership team who have responsibility for fundraising, finances, facilities, and so forth.

Vice President (Vice Chancellor)

As members of the senior leadership team, vice presidents/vice chancellors can hold a variety of responsibilities in their management roles. The level of vice president elevates the scope of the work from daily operations to more direct involvement in strategic planning and initiatives. Critics of the preponderance of vice presidents in higher education argue that the title is often awarded in lieu of a significant salary raise. Others note that the title is often associated *with* a higher salary (or raise if the position is filled internally), and during financially lean times, this is sometimes hard for academic community members to reconcile amidst budget cuts and programmatic reductions and refer to the positions as administrative bloat. Administrators defend the creation of these senior administrator positions in view of the escalating complexity of regulatory demands and need to have specialized expertise at a leadership level. Most institutions, for example, have added Vice Presidents of Diversity, Equity, Inclusion, and Justice as cabinet-level appointments.

Dean

The title of dean is most often associated with the leader of a specific school within a college or university. Academic deans are responsible for: ensuring students' successful progression through their programs; the budget, program development, and assessment; implementing strategic initiatives handed down from the provost and/or president; and executing other tasks required of those in positions of middle management. Deans are also involved in the hiring and evaluation for faculty members.

Faculty

Many faculty members express little to no desire to move into administrative roles. They love their academic disciplines and fields of study, and they are happiest learning along with the students they teach. Depending on the institution and the specific contract or workload agreement, some faculty members also have some administrative responsibility, such as a Program Director or Department Chair. This can create complications for faculty members who have to straddle faculty and "management" cultures without feeling fully connected to either realm. One faculty member in our study expressed this very phenomenon as "being on a lonely island" because while they signed a faculty contract agreement year to year, they are not allowed in the faculty union due to their oversight of "regular" faculty members. One of the reasons that faculty members remain faculty for many years, in spite of experiencing workplace frustrations, is that the vibrant academic setting inspires them to engage in creative activities (e.g., research, writing, visual arts, lab sciences) and establish relationships within and across their own disciplines and engage in service to their fields. The following terms relate to the culture of faculty.

Professor

This is the highest rank on a tenure track and at most institutions without tenure systems (see below). Full professors typically demonstrate accomplishments at the national and international levels and are recognized leaders in their disciplines. Some institutions have expectations for grant writing and scholarship that, over time, replace teaching requirements for academic workload.

Associate Professor

An assistant professor who has been awarded tenure, or successfully navigated a promotion process, typically advances to this rank. An associate professor is expected to have attained national recognition and to be involved in service and research beyond the scope of their institution.

Assistant Professor

This is the first, entry-level academic rank for a core faculty member ("core" is distinct from an "adjunct" faculty member who works on a course by course, non-tenure basis). In this rank, faculty are responsible for teaching, service (e.g., committee work within the institution and in the field), and scholarship, and faculty demonstrate different strengths in one or more of those areas year to year, as opportunities and interests evolve over time.

Instructor/Lecturer

An instructor/lecturer is a non-tenure-track teaching position, and people in these roles are often required to have attained an advanced degree, though not a terminal degree in their field (e.g., M.Ed. and no Ph.D.). Depending on the institutional practices and policies, instructors may teach more courses than "core" (permanent full-time) faculty members, and there are no research expectations for people in this role. Service activity is welcome and encouraged at the individuals' discretion and typically keeps people connected with their field.

Tenure

This term reflects a professional status for academics, whereby they have demonstrated accomplishments in teaching, research, publication/creative output, and service to the university and their field. A typical "tenure track" is a five- to seven-year period that begins when a faculty member starts teaching at their university, and a tenure committee reviews materials that are also reviewed by external parties who volunteer their time and provide formal feedback. A successful candidate is awarded tenure, which typically means permanent employment at their institution. Not all institutions have tenure systems, and some substitute long-term contract systems in which faculty members submit materials on a basis in accordance with their academic rank.

Union/Non-Union

Faculty who are part of a labor union are part of an organization that represents their collective interests around matters subject to "bargaining," such as salaries, workload, and other conditions of employment. At public institutions, unionization is based on state laws, whereas unionization at private institutions is guided by federal laws, including the United States Constitution. Unionization can include members in varying roles at an institution, such as staff, graduate student employees, adjunct faculty, and core faculty. The most positive attribute of unionization is the feeling of protection for faculty whose workplace environments are (or are perceived as) threatening, and the prevailing negative effect of unionization is the constraint that results from explicit, extremely detailed collective bargaining agreements (CBAs) that can hinder an institution's ability to be flexible or nimble.

Senate/Assembly

The terms Academic Senate or Faculty Assembly are commonly used to describe the academic or faculty governance structure at an academic institution. These systems offer different opportunities for faculty to be engaged, represented, and connected with administrators in efforts to effectively solve problems and strive to align academic efforts with the overall institutional mission.

We know that perceptions of people within groups (entitative) and outside of groups influence the interactions that occur in a variety of contexts. As authors of this book, whose professional relationship grew out of academic entitativity, we feel strongly that it is important to notice and cultivate opportunities when similarities – shared values, beliefs, and goals – can be harnessed to communicate and clarify common goals.

This is where intercultural communication is helpful. Shared interests and experiences provide moments to appreciate our own and others' humanity and establish personal connections. Communication opens pathways for administrators and faculty members to share frustrations with the cultural gaps that exist. Such mutual exchange works when administrators and faculty trust each other. Such trust takes root when people make intentional, often uncomfortable efforts to better know and understand each other. This can be as simple as a faculty member who disagrees with a decision made by a dean, and seeks further explanation to reduce concern. Similarly, a provost might feel frustrated by a faculty body's apparent lack of support for a decision and seek insight from faculty members, informally or through governance structures. We realize, of course, that most administrator–faculty relationships do not begin with the natural bonding experiences that we were lucky enough to have. That's why we argue that it is vitally important to be deliberate about it. In the sections that follow, we offer to readers a synthesis of feedback from the hundreds of participants in our research study, focus groups, and informal conversations with colleagues over decades of work in institutions of higher education. We have distilled perspectives into administrator and faculty amalgams, which communicate many parts into complex wholes. In this way, we are initiating communication about values, beliefs, and perceptions that can serve as insight you may use in your own settings and/or as provocation for further investigation.

THE ADMINISTRATOR PERSPECTIVE

Historically, administrators at the highest levels of leadership came out of academia – starting as faculty and working through the ranks. However, many administrators today have built careers and expertise related to business management and leadership at many kinds of organizations. This evolution is due, in part, to the increasingly complex nature of running an academic institution and the need for a wide range of leadership skills and experience. Administrators operate institutions that are facing constant challenges related to student admissions, human resources, campus environmental impact, community health and safety, and much more (Karabell, 2020). While many faculty members stay at one institution for years (possibly their whole careers), administrators typically change settings and roles more frequently. If they started as faculty members with a passion for a particular subject or field of study, they may have chosen to move into administration because they discovered a preference for helping advance academic programs and mentoring faculty rather than teaching students directly, or they may realize they'd rather influence the institution as a whole. The opinions presented below comprise, as noted previously, an amalgam.

INTRODUCING: ADMINISTRATOR "S"

Prior to becoming an administrator, I was a faculty member and found myself developing programs. I realized that I was good at it and had the capacity to motivate and inspire and get people on board. I started programs in my field and there was great satisfaction in the opportunity to have a bigger impact. I was driven by a desire to create support for faculty in delivering programs. In my role as an administrator, I always try to be the administrator that I wish I'd had: decisive, clear, authentic. If I make a mistake, I try to acknowledge it and say I was wrong and I am sorry. I am committed to trying to be real.

Vulnerabilities

As a senior administrator, you begin to realize that there are three main things that you are held accountable for: the money you raise, enrollment, and how you manage crises. As an administrator, depending on your role, you are in a fish bowl and you are constantly evaluated in the court of public approval. With the rise in use of social media, the missteps and failings of university administrators make that fishbowl more visible, and criticism can be swift and relentless.

Privileges

One of the perks of being in administration is that you can actually make decisions that influence the direction of academic issues. When you are a faculty member, you may see what could/should be done, but you don't get to decide. That's very frustrating. There is definitely tremendous satisfaction in being able to make decisions that will affect an outcome for good. It's an incredible privilege to be able to be in a leadership role and know that your decisions and actions have the capacity to impact lives. It feels weighty because of the huge responsibility. It's also frustrating, because many times others think that I can make a decision when in fact my hands are tied for a variety of political, legal, fiscal, or other reasons.

The decisions I make will impact an institution and whether or not the institution will thrive and be able to meet the needs of all these different stakeholders within our community: our students and our faculty and staff who rely on those livelihoods to support their families. My decisions ultimately impact many, many people. Also, families are going into debt for these degrees, so these degrees better position them for something. I also feel responsible for setting a culture where people are valued, a culture of respect and dignity, of openness and inclusion.

Frustrations

Administrators feel frustrated when faculty think that administrators have nefarious or devious intent. People often seem to think we are up to something or trying to undermine them. Usually, we are just dealing with complicated issues that have ramifications far beyond what any one faculty member can see, and we are often not at liberty to share the details that would give people a broader understanding of the situation (due to legal or other privacy restraints). Therefore, administrators sometimes believe that faculty don't understand the different constituents and stakeholders who must be kept appeased. Most administrators assume that faculty just don't get "it" – everything related to what it takes to keep an institution alive.

I wish faculty understood that our financial survival is not guaranteed. When we decide to teach out a program or re-allocate resources, we don't make those decisions lightly. We don't feel like faculty understand the magnitude of the challenges of keeping our institutions solvent, of how precarious things are in higher education. Faculty accuse us of "administrative bloat," but they don't realize the extent of the regulations we have to comply with (literally stacks of binders of regulations). All of this work requires investment, yet faculty see administrators as working against them.

Validation

The statements above stem from our own research findings and are also reflected at a national level. According to a recent study (American College President Study), 45% of participants identified "faculty resistance to change" as a top frustration. Furthermore, 57% said they think faculty possess the least understanding of institutional challenges compared to other constituent groups, such as deans, provosts, admissions staff, and department heads (American Council on Education's Center for Policy Research and Strategy, 2017).

THE FACULTY PERSPECTIVE

Based on the authors' own professional lives and combined years of work experience, and affirmed by research literature, people tend to become faculty members because they are intensely fascinated by a particular field of study and have built careers that allow them to deepen their knowledge and share their expertise with others. Faculty members also renew their own energy stores through the interactive process of teaching students and advising scholars. Some people prefer the research to the teaching, and others prefer the opposite.

Faculty are smart, inquisitive, and enjoy having autonomy. At times, this attitude can come across to administrators as "stay out of my way, I'll do what I want." Academic freedom is among the highest values embedded in faculty traditions and culture and is considered an important protection against totalitarianism. Faculty envision, build, and nurture courses and programs over time and are therefore very protective of them. That protection is understandable when you consider the time spent researching, teaching, and expanding on a beloved subject. If academic resources or territory is (or is perceived to be) threatened, or if faculty expertise is (or is perceived to be) underutilized and/or unappreciated, faculty are less inclined to cooperate with administrative initiatives.

INTRODUCING: FACULTY MEMBER "K"

I always thought I would find a job related to my college major and Master's degree field, but when I applied for jobs, I received such mediocre offers that I felt really dejected. It was after reading an issue of *Cosmopolitan* that I felt motivated to march into a publishing company's office building, ride the elevator to the children's literature floor, and ask to speak with the Children's Book editor. One thing led to another, and I wound up as an in-house temp, gaining brief experience that I put on my resume. That led to an editorial assistant gig at an academic press, where I spent a lot of time speaking with authors of textbooks, and I was inspired by how much they knew about their subject matter. I wanted to do what they did and be an expert in my field. After getting my Ph.D., I taught at one college for two years and then landed a job at my current university. I've been here for almost 20 years, and I've served on virtually every committee possible, taking on leadership positions time and again.

I've been a program chair, department chair, and had a stint as an interim administrator. I don't mind speaking up for faculty issues, and I know some administrators consider me "difficult" – or worse. A faculty colleague once told me that I "care too much." I can't imagine not caring, but now I do try to not get upset about things that I cannot control.

Vulnerabilities

Students sometimes love you or hate you and that's out of your control. But their social media posts, online reviews, and course evaluations are visible to many eyes. If students rip you to shreds, those reviews are out there, whether they're true or not, and there's no easy mechanism for rebuttal or clarification. A similar dynamic can exist with direct supervisors – if they don't like you, they can assign you to teach classes you don't want to teach or put you on a committee that's particularly intense. They can also manipulate administrative workload in ways that benefit some faculty members and burden others. There are definitely power cliques and dynamics that are hard to work with. Fortunately, faculty members tend to out-last terrible administrators, so the pain is temporary.

Privileges

Faculty are the ones who forge close, meaningful relationships with the students – and sometimes with their families – who can become colleagues, donors, or simply friends. These relationships are heartwarming and rejuvenating. There's also a lot of flexibility with my work schedule. There's a statement about teachers in general – "They get the summers off." – that reflects a lack of understanding of faculty worklife and scholarship, and that type of comment is aggravating when it's used in a pejorative sense.

There is something exhilarating about academic conferences, particularly national and international ones, where you get to meet others who are interested in the work that fills you up emotionally and intellectually. The research can sometimes end up with the 30,000-foot feel (only academics speaking to other academics in the "ivory tower"), but it can also have real impact on the ground, in applied settings. When you think about having a direct impact on human lives, there's nothing more meaningful.

Frustrations

Faculty appreciate it when people in positions of authority listen to us – truly consult us when they're making decisions that affect academic programs – and don't just pretend to consult us. Faculty also value humility. If you try something and it doesn't work, it's okay to admit it and then we can rethink it together. It is exceedingly frustrating when administrators think they know best when it comes to teaching and curriculum. Too often, it feels like the administrators make decisions without our input, or that we aren't given any context to understand how decisions fit into a larger plan or vision. So, then we end up creating our own narratives and tend to complain that administrators make changes too quickly and are too focused on money.

When administrators have never spent time as faculty, they don't have an appreciation for our challenges – like faculty workload or the fact that our careers progress as they do. For example, it's a fact that there are typically just two times in our careers when we can get raises. We don't often get compensated for directed studies, and we don't always receive mentoring. Administrative staff can move into different roles, get promoted, or reconfigure themselves on a different career track, and the advancement opportunities for faculty are much more limited unless you want to become a dean, provost, or president. But then you lose the best part of your job – the teaching and the relationships with students.

Validation

Faculty participants in our research study expressed, in surveys and focus groups, that they believe that most administrators have lost sight of the mission of education, prioritizing money and power over curiosity and humility – "moving fast down the wrong path." Approximately one in three faculty members indicated that they feel cut out of shared governance, with little or no voice in decisions that affect their ability to teach and support students.

On a positive note, a recent annual study (Professor Pulse, 2018) revealed that while they were forthright with frustrations related to funding, enrollment and retention, and other factors, faculty overwhelmingly intend to continue their careers in higher education. The top reasons cited were "I want to teach students" (72%) and "I want to continue to research in my field" (19%). The option "I plan to move into higher ed administration" was selected much less frequently (4%).

TRICKY, STICKY TRANSPARENCY

If administrators believe that faculty "don't get it," and faculty believe that administrators "don't tell us anything," then how can anyone expect to move through a frustrating stalemate? Nearly 25% of our faculty survey respondents cited lack of transparency or lack of openness as their biggest frustration with administrators. As presented in Chapter One, and reiterated in this chapter, understanding the perspectives of others who define themselves (or are perceived by the other) as a particular group or culture can help generate movement and build goodwill.

As administrators noted, there are often legal or other privacy concerns that constrain administrators and limit what they can say about a particular topic. One administrator in our study described the challenge of maintaining a balance between transparency and privacy when necessary:

> When you come to me with a concern, I wish you would know that I'm managing multiple conversations on the very point you're bringing up. I feel like I have to play dumb sometimes. I want faculty to be sensitive to the fact that if I'm sounding naïve on a topic, it's not always because I don't know about it or am naïve. I have to have a poker face. If there's something really sensitive that we're talking about, something may be hitting my 'administrator heart' but I can't reveal that in our conversation. If you hear me respond with 'Mmm-hmm,' just know that [it] means so many things. It may sound like a weak response sometimes, but there's so much complexity. Trust that the 'Mmm-hmm' may have more weight behind it.

On one hand, a leader's candor and honesty is refreshing. On the other hand, it's not always safe for the leader if their well-intentioned messages get shared out of context. Unintended legal issues can stem from the seemingly innocent sharing of information and can become a landslide of crisis management. This tension has been firmly established in research literature, as exemplified in the following statement:

> Openness in governance, upon systemic study, is both widely shared as a public value and hotly disputed in its application. Higher-education leaders honor its tenets in the abstract, and debate its

proper extensions in their day-to-day work. This duality cannot be condemned, for it is fully in keeping with the ambiguities of our democracy itself.

(McLendon & Hearn, 2006, p. 88)

Transparency can therefore incline people to be more hesitant to share and be vulnerable, because no one can control how whatever is shared will be received, interpreted, or tweeted.

WEIGHING THE RISKS OF VULNERABILITY

Administrators often struggle with this issue as they progress into leadership roles, believing that any displays of vulnerability won't be seen as professional. A focus group participant shared their experience in an early role, where they received the icy stares of colleagues when they thought they were just being authentic, and they learned to put on their administrative "armor" to protect themselves from those who would use their humanity against them. Over time, this individual learned how to be an administrator in their own way, and now lets their natural empathy come through when appropriate, but they also know that someone in their administrative role is not rewarded for being vulnerable. Such vulnerability can actually be a barrier to building trust with faculty *and* fellow administrators, but it's also a reality that this person chooses to navigate.

Research affirms this type of effort. Author Christine Fox (1997) suggests that "authenticity in a communicative situation is not superficial or easily come by. It is an honorable kind of conversation, based on mutual trust and respectful sharing of intended meanings" (p. 85). In her article, she poses provocative questions such as "Why should it be assumed that groups of people who identify themselves as of a different race, ethnic or cultural group, and whose discourse norms are different, cannot successfully communicate?" and "are there really such separate discourse norms for social interaction that cultural boundaries cannot be bridged?" (p. 86). Sometimes, the primary obstacle to bridging perceived gaps is the power dynamic that exists in the higher education context.

THE COMPLEX NOTION OF POWER

The source and exercise of power is not often clear cut. For example, the president of a university may have a lot of power by virtue of their role and the scope of their responsibilities. Faculty certainly perceive administrators to hold power and acknowledge this reality. But while a president has the authority to make certain decisions, they are also held accountable for those decisions and answers to multiple stakeholders demanding competing decisions. While it may appear that the president has the power to make certain choices, each choice has the potential to generate negative outcomes.

Sometimes, we don't want to understand another perspective because we are frustrated with the power differential. We resist and/or instinctively put up defenses because we resent the power difference, quite often when there is a miscommunication or a disagreement. If a faculty member doesn't agree with an administrator's decision, but doesn't have any power or influence to change the situation, is this truly an issue of clashing cultures? Is this a genuine misunderstanding? Or is someone exercising their power?

An administrator shared this perspective in the context of a focus group:

> There's something intoxicatingly sick about being in a senior leadership role where people are afraid to tell you what they think. Instead, they say what they think you want to hear and then they talk behind your back. It's isolating. I have to constantly remind myself that people are projecting onto me – they're not seeing me, they're seeing the power I represent, the perceived power that I have. I have to remind myself of what it was like for me when I was not in this position. It's easy to forget.

While faculty members may not wield the same amount of decision-making power in their institutional roles, as educators and advisors they influence students in profound ways. Administrators therefore perceive faculty as having a lot of power, or at least having more power than faculty tend to think. For example, within the tenure system, faculty can attain lifetime appointments. Those faculty who bring in large research grants or are connected with powerful donors or other resources can be perceived as "untouchable" to administrators, regardless of those faculty members' temperaments or collegiality.

The simple fact is that the question of who has power and who doesn't is an issue that can be investigated within each individual institution – sometimes many times and over time. When people representing different cultures attempt to understand each other – even if they're simultaneously trying to decide if it's worth trying to understand the other – they're working through the complicated issues of power and trust.

WHAT WE SHARE AND AGREE UPON

We began this chapter asking readers to guess whether an administrator or faculty member made a particular exclamation. We end this chapter in the same way, with the following quote from one of the participants in our research study:

"The majority of us believe that students are the most important reason for our existence."

At our core, administrators and faculty are united in what's best for students. Higher education contributes to society by providing students with equitable access to high-quality education that extends into vibrant careers upon graduation and therefore strengthens our nation's workforce. When administrators and faculty members lock horns, it delays progress, hampers innovation, and results in inefficiencies that distract us from meeting these fundamental goals. In challenging times, we can always return to a focus on teaching and learning practices and resources that contribute to this shared core value. This is a clarion call, and we have to work together. The future of higher education depends on it.

SUMMARY

This chapter introduced readers to the complex cultures of administrators and faculty and to the very notion of defining culture and facilitating communication between groups. Examples draw from research participants' statements (in the authors' research study), as well as decades of professional experience, and illustrate perceptions held by members of these groups. These concrete examples provide readers with insight into an unfamiliar cultural group and invite reflection and consideration of implications related to power and trust.

PRACTICE AND REFLECTION

1. Think of a few social groups that you belong to with which you feel a level of affinity or entitativity. What are some similarities among these groups and what are some differences related to how members of the groups behave and/or communicate. How do these groups contribute to your sense of identity in your workplace?
2. Think of a situation in which you experienced stress in your workplace. What were the causes or focus of the stress, and how did your position related to power impact your experience? Were there opportunities to engage in conversations with others who could provide an alternate perspective to your own? If so, what prevented you from or encouraged you to take these opportunities?
3. Consider a group that you have been a part of for a long time and how you have participated as a member of that group. What are the factors that provide a sense of belonging, and how might you invite

communication with others who are not currently members of this group? How do you think the comfort you experience can open avenues for conversation with others in your workplace setting?

RESOURCES

Global and Cultural Effectiveness: Belonging is the Missing Piece in the Fight for Inclusion

https://www.shrm.org/resourcesandtools/hr-topics/behavioral-competencies/global-and-cultural-effectiveness/pages/viewpoint-belonging-is-the-missing-piece-in-the-fight-for-inclusion.aspx

This webpage features and guides readers through workplace experiences and strategies that optimize opportunities for inclusion among community members.

Entitativity, as discussed by Dr. Anita Blanchard

https://pages.uncc.edu/anitablanchard/2019/09/18/an-entitativity-measure-and-why/

This webpage presents visitors with concrete visual examples to consider how we process groupness. There are links to additional resources for those who want to dig deeper into this psycho-social phenomenon.

How to Navigate a Turf War at Work

https://hbr.org/2017/09/how-to-navigate-a-turf-war-at-work

Advice from the Harvard Business Review is often sought by administrators at various organizations. This webpage presents case study and scholarly examples to elucidate concrete strategies that can move workplace colleagues through moments of tension and stalemate.

REFERENCES

American Council on Education's Center for Policy Research and Strategy. (2017). *American College President Study*. Retrieved at https://www.aceacps.org/

Fox, C. (1997). The authenticity of intercultural communication. *International Journal of Intercultural Relations, 21*(1), pp. 85–103.

Jhangiani, R., & Tarry, H. (2019). Understanding social groups. *Principles of Social Psychology: 1st International Edition*. Retrieved at https://opentextbc.ca/socialpsychology/chapter/understanding-social-groups/

Karabell, Z. (2020, August 27). The economic model of higher education was already broken: Here's why the pandemic may destroy it for good. *Time*. Retrieved at https://time.com/5883098/higher-education-broken-pandemic/

McLendon, M.K., & Hearn, J.C. (2006). Mandated openness and higher-education governance. In J.C. Smart (Ed.), *Higher education: Handbook of theory and research* (Vol. XXI). Springer.

Piller, I. (2012). Intercultural communication: An overview. In C.B. Paulston, S.F. Kiesling, & E.S. Rangel (Eds.), *The handbook of intercultural discourse and communication*. John Wiley & Sons.

Rosowsky, D.V., & Hallman, K. (2020, May 20). Communicating culture in a distributed world. *Inside Higher Ed*. Retrieved at https://www.insidehighered.com/views/2020/05/26/importance-culture-binding-higher-ed-institution-together-during-crises-pandemic

Top Hat. (2018). *Professor Pulse*. Retrieved at https://tophat.com/wp-content/uploads/Professor-Pulse-Full-Report-Top-Hat.pdf

Chapter Three

The Urgency: Higher Education Is Fighting for Survival

Enrollments are down, institutions have become commoditized, degrees don't guarantee careers with a living wage, tuition outpaces inflation, political criticism abounds, and a college education is no longer assumed to be worth the tremendous debt accrued by students and families. These are challenges that institutions of higher education were facing *before* the COVID-19 pandemic.

At the time we are writing this book, still in the midst of global pandemic, a perusal of headlines from the archives of academic publications provides a glimpse into the depth of the uncertainty about the future of academia before and during the COVID-19 pandemic (e.g., García & Weiss, 2020). Table 3.1 provides a sampling of headlines from *The Chronicle of Higher Education* that, while perhaps designed to grab readers' attention, reflect the challenges and priorities for institutions of higher education in recent years.

These challenges and priorities are the source of many of the disagreements related to the cultures of faculty and administrators. Everyone wants their institution to survive. But what does that mean? What does survival look and feel like? What kinds of changes are tolerable in pursuit of survival?

There's the threat of extinction – the opposite of survival – intensified by the economic realities resulting from the Great Recession of 2008 (Long, 2012) and the global pandemic that rocked the world in 2020. There's also the threat of assimilation – a survival of the soul – made more difficult when considering the compromises an institution might be forced to make in order to ensure its viability and sustainability.

In spite of many faculty members' ardent wishes to the contrary, institutions of higher education are, in fact, businesses. Therefore, it is to the business realm that academic leaders turn when seeking advice and insights that will help their institutions thrive. Two business professors, writing in *The Harvard Business Review*, recently called for university

Table 3.1 Higher Education Headlines

Headlines pre-pandemic	Headlines during COVID-19 crisis
Private Colleges Say They Aren't Just for the Rich	The Coronavirus Enrollment Crash
In 2015, the Most Famous Bovine in College Sports	Are Colleges Ready for a Different Kind of Teaching this Fall?
A University Confronts the Email Deluge, for Students' Sake	How will the Pandemic Change Higher Education?
As Campus Gun Violence Increases, So Do Professors' Fears	Under COVID-19, University Budgets Like We've Never Seen Before
Colleges Have Spent Big Money on Innovation Centers. Do They Work?	For Tiny Colleges, Federal COVID-19 Stimulus Is a Windfall

leaders to "use what they are learning in crisis now to position their institutions for greatest impact in the decades to come" (Govindarajan & Srivastava, 2020, par. 4), arguing that the current pandemic crisis creates opportunities to remake institutions. This notion of remaking during and after a crisis is not new, and whether the crisis is biological or economic in nature, the urgency is real.

NO SIGNAL

It's hard to navigate institutional territory during a crisis, because the old road maps aren't always useful – an analogy similar to how many people now use Waze or Google maps on their smartphones to follow someone (or something) else's instructions about where to go when we're walking or driving. Almost 50 years ago, Ernest Boyer (known well in academic circles for his work defining categories of scholarship) wrote an article titled, *We Must Find New Forms for Higher Education* (1972). His words ring true today, in spite of the tremendous advances that have been experienced in higher education on many levels, which we will discuss in the sections that follow. Boyer wrote:

> All this would be merely an exercise in rather curdled nostalgia were it not for the fact that so much of what took shape in that earlier time still survives today. This model of the self-contained campus – well-rooted in the circumstance of the time – has been locked into an iron vise of custom and still forms our image of 'the way things used to be.' And while our world has been transformed around us, we still cling to a mental picture of higher education…

> We are, in short, in one of those periods of lag, in which an institution evolves more slowly than the society it serves.
>
> (par. 12)

This article is all the more striking because Boyer identified the "[m]illions of Americans...now looking for new educational approaches that reflect the changing realities of our time" (par. 13), and the article was published three years before the first personal computers were introduced and available to the public (a.k.a., anyone who could assemble the parts that comprised the microcomputer electronic kits). In the time that has passed between the publication of that article and the publications of this book, the following events have occurred and impacted citizens:

- The United States Supreme Court passed the landmark *Roe v. Wade* decision (1973)
- The U.S. Centers for Disease Control and Prevention published a report about what we now know as HIV/AIDS (1981)
- The "greatest street party in the history of the world" occurred when the Berlin Wall came down (1989)
- The dotcom bubble began to swell, driven by investments in Internet-based companies and increased U.S. technology stock values (1995)
- The euro entered into circulation, becoming the official currency (thereby replacing the former currencies) of 19 of the 27 member countries of the European Union (2002)
- President Barack Obama was elected, becoming the first African American President of the United States (2009)
- The deadliest wildfires in California history caused over $3 billion of damage and inestimable emotional grief and trauma (2018)
- The COVID-19 pandemic emerged and spread throughout the world, contributing to almost 4 million deaths and inestimable emotional and financial damage (as of June 2021)

While the "changing realities" of the present time for higher education are very much entangled in technology and the related issues of privacy, access, and integrity, it is important to note the existence of many contextual factors that fall outside the realm of "education," but very much impact the education domain.

It is therefore no wonder that the field of higher education is going through its own identity crisis as individual institutions seek to reassert or redefine their campus cultures, yet again, to meet the needs of citizens and simultaneously fulfill the missions that birthed the institutions. In the sections that follow, we share some of the challenges that create tensions between faculty and administrators – two constituent groups passionately and distinctly invested in the stability and growth of their institutions, and whose cultural perspectives are at times harmonious and other times at odds.

MODALITY MATTERS

Throughout our research study, we asked participants to share what they see as the biggest decisions that will need to be made about the future of higher education, the future of their respective institutions, and/or the future of their professions. Their statements affirmed sentiments expressed by workplace colleagues and professional conference attendees over several decades. Furthermore, research literature validates the viewpoints and compass needle that inclines members of faculty and administrator cultures toward certain viewpoints. One of the most-often cited points of contention was the category we have identified as "modality." The way that a course is delivered is a very serious topic, for reasons that differ for people based on their philosophical and pedagogical stance.

Online Learning and Face-to-Face Instruction

The subject of online learning originally gained traction primarily because of the way it could provide access to populations that had previously been less able to enter higher education contexts, such as adult learners and/or people with less income to spend on high tuition rates. The delivery model quickly gained appeal, as many products do, due to the ability for courses to be designed once and then offered widely and often through online platforms. One of the first, and consistently referenced, voices to prophesize the impact that online learning offerings would have on high education was Harvard Business School professor Clay Christensen. In 2017, Christensen warned that "online education will become a more cost-effective way for students to receive an education, effectively undermining the business models of traditional institutions and running them out of business" (Hess, 2018, par. 3). This warning was made more explicitly dire with Christensen asserting his belief that half of American colleges and universities will be bankrupt in 10 to 15 years (he lessened the window to nine or ten years when pressed further while giving a subsequent presentation).

Christensen gained acclaim with his theory of "disruptive innovation," which suggests that "certain kinds of cheaper, usually inferior innovations change an industry not by serving current consumers better, but by greatly broadening the audience willing and able to consume that product or service" (Lederman, 2017, par. 1). This argument is precisely what those who resist developing online courses argue – that the quality is inferior to that of face-to-face instruction. This tension shifted when the global pandemic forced institutions of higher education to rapidly transition many courses to online delivery, and some faculty found a surprising number of tools and resources that enhanced the online experience and which they plan to retain and integrate into their face-to-face delivery when pre-COVID activities can safely resume. Many administrators found a tremendous relief in the unexpected detente in the modality stand-off and hope that it is not just a temporary stretch in faculty opinion.

In a conversation with Dr. Sanjay Gupta, Professor Scott Galloway of the Stern School of Business at NYU offered his opinions about how the pandemic could "disrupt" (echoing Christensen's [2017] term) the public's perceived value of higher education:

> ...I would largely or loosely just articulate the value into three components: The first is the certification. The second factor is the education you receive. And then the final one is the experience. It's those three things over the price. Now because the prices have escalated so dramatically, that ratio no longer yields an automatic yes.
>
> (Gupta, 2020, par. 8)

Venturing further, Professor Galloway predicts that "big tech" companies like Apple and Google are going to reinforce the expansion of online learning in higher education:

> ...I think big tech is going big-game hunting. And the biggest game out there are two industries: education and US health care. So I don't think big tech goes into education and health care because they want to; I think they go into it because they have to.
>
> (par. 36)

Yet, in spite of the financial appeal for institutions of higher education and students alike – increased access to coursework at a reduced cost, therefore greatly increasing revenue while keeping overhead to a minimum – Professor Galloway does note aspects of face-to-face, on-campus learning:

> Having all of these [developmental milestones] happen in a safe, joyous place is wonderful. It's just — it's an extraordinary experience. So I agree that, that the nonquantitative benefits here, the, the opportunity to spill into adulthood in a safe, joyous place and to explore topics outside of your, maybe your career interests that

create empathy, that create curiosity, that's an amazing thing. It's an amazing thing.

(par. 22)

And thus the questions about course modality in higher education reveal no clear answers, and the debate remains vigorous among faculty, administrators, and researchers who have found fertile ground to dig into the perpetual pursuit of best practices in changing times (e.g., Gallagher & Palmer, 2020; Rapanta et al., 2020; Whillans et al., 2020).

FACULTY PERSPECTIVES

Depending on the discipline, faculty members are more or less inclined to teach in an online format. It is difficult, for example, to recreate a science lab or an art studio experience online, and yet faculty members have found creative ways to guide instruction utilizing lab kits and lists of art materials that facilitate students' learning that is complemented with online teaching and technology. Faculty teaching dance therapy classes or American Sign Language have utilized tools that they would not have chosen to use before the pandemic. Forced into a choice between no teaching and online course conversion, some faculty have been extremely surprised and pleased with the advances that technology affords.

Studies conducted before the pandemic resounding underscored faculty members' and students' preferences for face-to-face instruction (e.g., Koenig, 2019). During the academic terms that have occurred since COVID-19 forced school closures and transformations, opinions have moved to a more moderate place. Consider the following comments made by faculty members:

- Online teaching lets me be more student-centered. Every student has different ways of learning – some prefer the anonymity that some tools provide, and they can share opinions without worrying about judgment or criticism, using discussion boards or class polls.
- There are no field trips that are out of reach anymore – I can take students to visit caves in Vietnam or the British Museum! Virtual tools and tours are free and accessible any time. We don't need to worry about permissions, liability, transportation, or any of those things. The world and its wonders are literally a click away. These experiences enrich our class discussions and help us build community.

And yet, with the benefits that online instruction can provide to teaching and learning, many faculty express a variation on the following sentiment:

- I can't wait to be back in the classroom with students again. It's what I love about teaching – reading their body language, the moment-to-moment twists and turns that take us somewhere I'd never have planned. I don't think it's possible to form the same kinds of relationships with students in an online setting. Especially with students who never turn their camera on, someone could walk up to me on the street and I wouldn't recognize them. Something is definitely lost.

ADMINISTRATOR PERSPECTIVES

Leaders in higher education settings perennially argue that their institutions must be "on the cutting edge" or invested in "innovation" to remain competitive in a landscape that promises graduates will be able to demonstrate 21st century skills. These skills, curiously all "c"-words such as collaboration, communication, critical thinking, and career-ready, are vague enough to prompt initiatives and financial investments, yet also vague enough to frustrate administrators attempting to convince faculty constituents of the merits of certain pursuits.

Administrators, accountable to numerous competing entities and committed to advancing the institution's mission, sometimes find themselves straddling a thorny fence as they attempt to retain the historical culture and spirit of their setting while shining a light forward into unfamiliar directions. Consider the following comments made by administrators:

- We have to re-imagine what it is like to learn. Look back to electricity and light: if we only ever imagined having candles, we wouldn't have the light bulb. We have to re-envision. It's exciting that we're being forced to re-imagine and re-envision. Those who are doing this will be those that emerge from this in different ways. Our oversight bodies also will have to re-imagine the ways they operate with us.
- College is more than a job lubricant. We're not just here to help people to get jobs. I know jobs are important. But I have to tell you, regarding the value of higher education in general, you can enter a number of fields without a college degree and be successful and maybe even have an affluent life. But knowledge, enlightenment, perspective, balance, diversity – those are things that a college education provides people that they might not get on another route.
- I wish faculty would understand that sometimes I need to make a business decision, and the timing of it means that I wasn't able to discuss it thoroughly with them to identify every possible piece of the puzzle. It doesn't have to be all or nothing – we can have

'blended' learning experiences that bring the best of both worlds into the learning experience.

There are many attractive features of online learning that can enhance what's best about an institution's academic offerings without compromising the quality of the instruction. One of the most compelling arguments relates to accessibility.

ACCESSIBILITY MATTERS

While the so-called "brick and mortar" buildings that are the visual hallmarks of higher education will likely stand the test of time, the challenges of affordability and physical access to post-secondary learning (due to myriad complicated factors) are among the most urgent for faculty and administrators to resolve. These challenges, if met with a commitment to collaborative problem-solving and resource allocation, can become opportunities to "unlearn unhelpful habits, and discard behavioral patterns" (Roper, 2019, p. 22).

Quality and Quantity

With institutions of higher education facing greater financial challenges to survival, perhaps more than ever before in their history, opportunities to increase access to instruction have the obvious "sticker appeal." If faculty and administrators agree upon the quality of their product, then the tensions are fewer if one or both parties decide to increase the number of offerings, specifically through online channels. Research into how stakeholders communicate in higher education settings reinforces ideas and information presented in Chapter Two:

> Unfortunately, the habitual ways that leaders and group conveners engage in conversation and the contexts they set for conversations do not produce the desired positive outcomes. The ingrained cultural approaches to conversations at most institutions do not consider the diverse needs, hopes, expectations, and values participants bring to the conversation.
>
> (p. 19)

Faculty members, largely due to their closer proximity to students, are aware of some challenges that students experience accessing courses. There is a range of challenges that includes physical, cognitive, social, and financial obstacles that students encounter. For example, a visually impaired student may not be able to access course content. Attempts to remedy this can include formal accommodations from offices associated with academic advising, disability services, and/or student retention, and these processes can sometimes take a long time – especially when human resources are stretched thin. In another example, a student may have a financial "hold" on their account, which prevents them from registering for classes during the cyclical registration period. They may therefore have no choice but to register late, perhaps during an academic "add/drop" period, and this sets them at a disadvantage because they will need to catch up on work missed, and they may not have funds to purchase required textbooks (or pay fees to access online materials associated with a class). Students may be juggling multiple, competing responsibilities associated with work, family, and self-care. These factors, while acutely known by faculty, are typically not as familiar to administrators who may most often learn about these challenges when problems arise.

Academic leaders frequently rely on others to communicate their thoughts to faculty and staff, because an institution's size makes it less common for faculty and administrators to engage in personal, individual conversations. This reality, along with administrators often mired in the "problems" than in the more frequent "successes," contributes to the disconnect that exists when decisions are made about program and class delivery.

> Sometimes messages do not get conveyed by intermediaries in the way the originator intended. E-mail...receives praise for its ability to reach numerous people instantly, but it can come across as impersonal and cold in the absence of voice tone or body language.
> (Griffith, 2006, p. 72)

As administrators build muscle, developing their eye for detail and inspiring institutional effectiveness, faculty members may be unaware of the competing demands on administrators' time. Building predictable opportunities into academic schedules for representatives from different groups to engage in conversation can, over time, reduce bias toward other groups. Researchers emphasize specific conditions that are vital to such intergroup communication: "equal status, common goals, intergroup cooperation, and the support of authorities" (Belet, 2018, p. 54). As you read the following perspectives expressed by faculty and administrators, see if you can identify opportunities to provide or nurture these conditions.

Faculty Perspectives

Faculty members who were drawn to higher education because of a love of learning about their particular discipline can find it difficult to change their pedagogical strategies in order to meet demands for access to less-expensive, more readily accessible courses. Faculty appreciate it when their advice is sought, or they are consulted about potential decisions before they are made, as time allows. Faculty can feel more sympathetic toward administrators when they see their input and expertise reflected in the outcomes of a discussion, even if it's not the outcome they would have preferred.

- We're not in the business of making widgets. If we keep up this pace, we're going to be nothing more than a factory, churning out cookie-cutter courses that have no flavor. We're a distinct institution with over 100 years of history that makes us who we are, and we're going to lose that if we enter the competitive landscape just to play the game.
- How can we possibly teach the same class in a 15-week, 8-week, face-to-face, hybrid, and completely online format? That doesn't make any sense. Students are going to want the quick and dirty class so that they can get through their program and get a job, but we don't want to compromise quality just to bend to the wishes of a population that just wants a quick degree. For-profit colleges have made this much more difficult.

Administrator Perspectives

Administrators can feel underappreciated because they are caught in the middle of a complicated network of accountability, inside and outside of the institution. It may surprise some faculty to know that many administrators yearn for more opportunities to provide mentorship and support to faculty and staff in their institutions. More frequent, informal opportunities for establishing connections can lay the groundwork for trust when difficult decisions or situations arise.

- Parents and families constantly ask me to explain whether or not our tuition is worth the investment. There are enrollment pressures and expectations from the board that make it very complicated when it comes to working out the equation – lots of variables and factors to consider!
- I have to find a way to convince people that I'm not in this for my ego or political gain, but town hall meetings either feel like heavy-handed 'appear upon demand' meetings or else people think they're just for show, checking off a box. If we are going to 'walk the talk,' we need to think outside the box so that more students can get access to education. There's a tangible commitment to equity and

inclusion that means more supports and that means more money spent to hire people to ensure that these needs are met.

In the section that follows, we discuss the complicated topic of money – one of the most challenging and heated topics that can be expected in virtually any institution of higher education.

MONEY MATTERS

Many different cultural groups in higher education bring varying perspectives to conversations about money – these perspectives reflect opinions about what money should be spent, how it should be spent, by whom, and how institutions of higher education are (or should be) held accountable for their spending. Over the past 50 years, there has been a marked increase in administrative spending, which has raised some eyebrows and concerns among university community members. The term "administrative bloat" emerged to describe the inflation that exists in higher education in the upper echelons of the institution, as people skeptically weighed the reality of the spending against the perceived return on investment.

Current arguments that purport to explain the reasons for spending include "a shifting landscape in higher education, including government regulations, competition between schools, and a modern population of students with increasing needs" (Simon, 2017, par. 9). In order to comply with increased regulations, staff must be hired to do the work, and this costs money in terms of salary and benefits. There are also expenses related to behind-the-scenes work that is fundamentally less visible to the public, connected to legal counsel or threat assessment costs. These are combined with the very much visible, highly publicized expenses related to health and wellness services, state of the art dining and recreation facilities, and more, all designed to attract students and support tuition-dependent institutions.

Another phenomenon that is similar to what educators and administrators experience in the public pre-K-12 arena is that society expects schools to manage many of the responsibilities long-held by families. Students who enter higher education programs are more diverse than in previous times, and this includes students who are first-generation college students, international students, and students who have a thoughtfully organized support system (including therapeutic and/or medical assistance) that provides them with stability previous generations of would-be prospective students would have wished for, but didn't exist. All of these students might benefit from academic and career advising, financial aid and planning, small class sizes, and robust extra-curricular opportunities. And all of these require a financial base in order to operate.

Revenue Generation and Not-for-Profit

The majority of institutions of higher education are not-for-profit organizations, yet the salaries of many upper-tier administrators is in the same range as that of Chief Executive Officers and Chief Operating Officers in the private sector. So, while the institutions are not organized around a profit model, they are organized around an implicit model that values sustainable, revenue-generating practices. When fiduciary responsibility rests primarily with a board of advisors/directors/trustees, and the board interacts primarily with the upper administration, there is an obvious relationship between spending habits and perceptions of high-need areas that sometimes manifest as buildings as opposed to hiring faculty and staff. Furthermore, trends reported in the business media outlets, typically followed closely by board members and administrators, can influence administrative initiatives that aim to increase revenue with less regard to the pedagogical implications. Professor Galloway, cited earlier, underscores the appeal of such decision-making:

> If you took half your learning online, you kind of effectively double the size of the campus. You double the capacity.
>
> So, I do think there's opportunity for our large land-grant public universities to cut costs, leverage technology and for taxpayers to recognize the importance of education and reallocate more capital while holding these universities accountable on cost per student and dramatically expand the freshman seats at some of these outstanding universities.
>
> (Gupta, 2020, par. 15)

The tug-of-war between investing in priorities that are "on the ground" (e.g., classroom technology, staff, faculty) versus ones that are less visible (e.g., directors of support offices, consultations with compliance experts) is one that accurately reflects the digging in and grunting and sweating that typically occurs in many institutions. As faculty and administrators attempt to find common ground, they are striving to return to a focus on providing students with knowledge and skills to happily and successfully engage in the world after they graduate.

Faculty Perspectives

Faculty recognize the commitment they share with administrators to support students, yet very often feel shut out of important decisions related to budget and planning. As a result of feeling vulnerable and confused, there is a positional stance that exists where many faculty seek to understand, but are already skeptical about what they are told. They report feeling certain that they are not told the "whole story."

- Because of COVID-19, there is a financial crisis in our school. So, many courses [were] cancelled for lack of students. This is disappointing because we have many first-year students who need to have that group connection that is hard to obtain virtually. We're losing that connectivity with our students. First-generation students are thirsty and hungry to have a relationship with faculty. There hasn't been a conversation about it, decisions have been made quite abruptly. We care deeply for our students but haven't seen that from the administration.
- The elephant in the room: we have to solve the tuition problem. We're just way too expensive. I didn't grow up in this country. I come from a place where families don't save money to send their kids to college; it's free or close to free. It's a problem we need to solve. It's almost one of those huge problems – like movies with aliens – where we have to fight a common enemy. The structure of higher ed, that it has to be so expensive – that's the common enemy. It's a huge problem. It's not sustainable.
- Accessibility, the costs to students. [We] can't adapt well when crises hit. One thing that COVID-19 has highlighted is a need for a system that meets students and faculty where they are. In a way that the full-time four-year, very expensive model does. I'd love to see it re-imagined in a way that's more affordable in terms of money and time. It makes me think of the other institutions we interface with. Federal student aid is only offered to students who are full-time…so we have to adapt all of the interfacing systems to a new model. I'm hoping COVID will actually crack open a bit. People could mourn the death of classic four-year, or we could celebrate the opportunity to re-imagine it.

Administrator Perspectives

When administrators attempt to demonstrate the value of their shared work with institutional colleagues, they receive most support when they establish a clear framework of how capital is more than mere dollars and cents. There is the "familial" capital that exists because of the relationships that institutional members have with each other, with students and families, and with community members. There is "aspirational" capital that exists in the hopes and expectations that students enter with and graduate with, based on the perceived value and marketing promises of an institution or specific program. All of these matter to different constituents for different reasons.

- Despite our long relationship with each other, or maybe because we have a level of comfort with each other due to the long relationship, there have been some really painful moments that we have encountered during committee meetings, bordering on insubordination. We never discuss these conflicts afterward and never process them as a community. I assume it's because we don't have a track record of communicating in this way and because of the power differential.
- In many ways, our institutional reputation has been coasting along on decades of past performance, and we need to create a strong "present" level of performance to sustain our future in this competitive landscape. We need to both be ourselves and also be able to change with the increasing diversity of the student body. I wish I could freeze time sometimes, so that I can catch up and highlight what makes us a powerful academic institution.

Research has touted the importance of diversity in an academic setting, pointing to positive effects associated with "problem-solving skills, interracial interaction, civic engagement, intellectual self-confidence, complex thinking, and satisfaction" (Sulé, 2011, p. 169). The field of higher education is currently struggling with the same challenges that our global society is facing related to racism, discrimination, and the lack of large measures of empathy, and compassion. If institutions of higher education are invested in the capacity of human and positive progress, then the heart and soul of society is intrinsically woven with higher education's search for identity.

IDENTITY MATTERS

Consider all of the challenges presented in this chapter and how higher education has remained a valued social institution:

> Whether in person or online, colleges and universities are safe spaces for self-exploration and self-expression, while sitting at the tip of the spear for diversity, access and inclusion, and integration conversations. They are builders of community and common ground, even when physical locations are dispersed, and they prepare young people to dialogue through differences and across distances. They are our most successful incubators of ideas, innovations and social

and scientific breakthroughs – where schools of thought become the seedlings of change. And certainly, they are major employers and economic drivers.

(Rosowsky & Hallman, 2020, par. 20)

In spite of the challenges, humans' capacities to develop and learn remain strong, and higher education faculty and administrators have made strides in the past two years that have been long overdue, with a long way yet to go, to be sure. In order to truly be welcoming communities for all members of any academic environment, race, culture, language, ability, trauma, and poverty are some of the topics that must be made more visible in curriculum, human and material resources, and investments made on behalf of an institution. In the sections that follow, we provide some insight into faculty and administrators' perspectives into community cultural capital.

Racism and Retention

The murder of George Floyd in 2020 and the protest movement that followed were the inter-related catalysts for a "reckoning" in many organizations across the United States, and many institutions of higher education initiated systemic efforts to confront racism, privilege, and bias. Some recommendations for "concrete steps" (Collymore, 2020) for institutions of higher education included:

- Require implicit-bias training for anyone involved in admissions
- Guarantee financial aid beyond the first year
- Require de-escalation training for public-safety officers
- Adopt a transparent student protest policy
- Conduct a campus-wide review of building and school names
- Create a strategic plan to hire a diverse faculty and staff
- Diversify health and wellness personnel
- Expand the scope of your chief diversity officer
- Engage in proactive dialogue

As may be expected when there is response to public outcry, some efforts will be fueled by an authentic desire for justice and equity, while others may be perceived as performative actions to protect an institution's reputation. Some people will welcome changes and others will fight them.

Many community members working and learning in higher education acknowledge that intentional institutional efforts to confront structural racism are important, and concrete steps provide clarity about where to begin for many institutions (especially ones that have never engaged in such work). Many people also recognize and emphasize that completing a checklist of items is not enough – learning and subsequent behavioral change is not a linear process. The process is one that takes time and requires a long-term commitment to examine systems that maintain oppressive "-isms." Such work challenges institutions to retain employees and students while they endeavor to maintain their responsiveness and meet the expectations of the general public.

Efforts related to diversity, equity, inclusion, and justice (DEIJ), safe spaces/courageous conversations, perceptions and realities, and decolonization across the campus are particularly important to students, who tend to believe that administrators aren't working hard enough or quickly enough to mobilize meaningful, tangible change.

> Students are torn on whether BLM has resulted in their institutions being a better place, with the highest percentage of survey respondents (33 percent) neither agreeing nor disagreeing. Only 6 percent strongly agree, and 15 percent strongly disagree. Broken out by race, results are similar, except with Native American students, who are far more likely to agree at least somewhat (56 percent), compared to 22 percent of students overall.
>
> (Ezarik, 2021)

Faculty have engaged students in collaborative efforts to decolonize curricula and learn about their art holdings and other collections. Many administrators have hired consultants to conduct land studies so they can learn about and share the history of the land upon which their buildings stand, followed by a commitment to making explicit how their institution has benefitted from the oppression of Indigenous peoples. "Colleges and universities are among the few places where people of different racial, cultural, and socioeconomic backgrounds can engage with each other in more than just a superficial way" (Tatum, 2019, p. 80). Of critical importance is for institutions of higher education to provide structures and resources for such interactions and learning experiences to occur and continue over time.

Faculty Perspectives

Some faculty enter the higher education arena with previous knowledge and skills that help them address racism and oppression in their classes, regardless of class content. Many faculty feel very unprepared to have difficult conversations with students, sometimes due to fear of parents' ire, or course evaluations that could be detrimental to their contract renewal or promotion, or simply because they don't want to say or do the "wrong thing." As we will continue to explore together in the chapters that follow, working from a starting point of trust sets the stage for meaningful conversations. The following statements from faculty members related to anti-racism and faculty development reveal a commitment to the work and an uncertainty about process:

- I think that I am currently on a path of un-learning. I have been reading so much and watching webinars and listening to podcasts, and now I am noticing so many things that I just accepted as 'the way it is' before. We went through an accreditation visit this year and had to provide evidence to document what [the accrediting organization] told us to provide, and I realized that the organization we're hoping to impress is asking us to use rubrics that perpetuate inequities that we keep talking about as so harmful to generations of people. I wanted to flip the table and rush out of the room.
- Students wrote many angry posts on social media about professors' and administrators' racist behaviors. I call it the 'dump and run' technique because there's no opportunity for dialogue – just a one-way rant. I invited students to join our department in a conversation between faculty and students, and two students showed up. It's so frustrating when students viciously complain anonymously but then aren't willing to do the hard work of being vulnerable together in a conversation. Maybe they're afraid? I don't know.

Administrator Perspectives

Administrators grapple with many of the same personal and professional doubts and confusion experienced by faculty. Administrators have the power to initiate campus-wide efforts and to allocate resources to hire faculty and staff who identify as Black, Indigenous, People of Color (BIPOC). They also have the accountability and the vulnerability if trainings are not well-received, or if employees are not met with favorable response by community members. Some administrators are comfortable stepping out of their comfort zone, while others fear that any vulnerability is a sign of weakness that will undermine their position and responsibilities.

- I'm wondering how I can sustain the engagement of our community without seeming too top-down. I'm so tired of being the target of every discontented employee or parent. I just had a call today from an angry parent, demanding that a faculty member doesn't show a certain video in a class because it presents the Middle East conflict in a way that he doesn't like. If students don't feel comfortable here,

that's something I cannot abide, but I can't give in to every parent's preferences.
- I think that we have some good momentum going. We've had panels, dialogue, and online experiences with presentations and role plays. I have no idea if this is trickling down into the students' awareness, though. I know that it's human nature to seek out people you're comfortable with because they're familiar. It's natural. I hope that students all feel like they at least belong here, even if they have a fairly homogeneous group of friends. They were drawn to us because something made them feel like they belong, and I want it to stay that way so they stay here.

RE-ENVISIONING THE LANDSCAPE

Faculty and administrators share the same goal: doing what's best for students. Universities are known for changing at a glacial pace. While that's frustrating, it's also comforting for faculty and administrators who hope that their institutions are around for another 100 years or more. Higher education is under intense scrutiny across many domains, and it will take creativity and persistence to adjust programs accordingly and maintain integrity and to demonstrate fidelity to the mission of the institution. Faculty and administrators are constantly planning for the students of tomorrow, while protecting what is precious about the institution for alumni, and simultaneously making sure that current students feel valued. When these two groups join forces, the tasks are stronger and the results are longer-lasting. Chapter Four presents information that we hope will inspire intercultural communication and collaboration in your workplace setting.

SUMMARY

Institutions of higher education have faced many challenges for decades. Areas that require constant vigilance and care include: revenue and tuition, student enrollments, keeping up with increasing regulations for compliance, modality debates, and finding sustainable, meaningful ways to increase diversity and maintain resources for DEIJ. Faculty and administrators are united in their desire to support their institutions' survival and to help all students feel safe, welcome, and valued in their campus community.

PRACTICE AND REFLECTION

1. One of the areas that faculty and administrators often complain about is lack of marketing or inaccurate representation of academics

in marketing materials. Do you have any experience developing a marketing plan or campaign? If so, describe what worked well in your process and/or materials.
2. Many administrators initiate a "strategic plan" shortly after they arrive at an institution, and long-time faculty members may go through several strategic planning processes during their tenure. What is an encouraging innovation or experience that came out of a strategic planning process where you work? What were some of the goals articulated in the plan, and how were resources allocated to support the work?
3. Describe the general hiring process at your workplace. Are there measures in place to ensure that job descriptions attract a diverse pool of applicants who will be considered fairly, without bias, to the greatest extent possible? *or* What can you commit to do to ensure that anti-racist and/or decolonializing curricula are introduced into students' programs and general education experiences?

RESOURCES

The #BuddleHuddle Podcast

https://www.mcgill.ca/deanofstudents/podcast

This podcast focuses on how the Dean of Students at McGill University creates community and builds relationships with the students and community members. Issues of primary importance to students are presented, and the website features explicit evidence of systemic DEIJ practice, such as a land acknowledgment and link to the office's anti-racism message.

Diversity, Equity, and Inclusion at BCG: Our U.S. Report

https://www.bcg.com/en-us/about/about-bcg/us-diversity-equity-inclusion-report

If academic leaders and business professors tend to appreciate the predictions made by experts in the business field, then this video provides a rich example of how employees at one of the most successful business organizations around the world participate together in training that elevates their work as a whole.

An Overview of Higher Education in the United States

https://www.acenet.edu/Documents/Overview-of-Higher-Education-in-the-United-States-Diversity-Access-and-the-Role-of-the-Marketplace-2004.pdf

This publication provides detailed coverage of many topics that have existed in higher education for decades or more. Many of the controversies presented in this chapter will be familiar to faculty and administrators and can be useful for group discussions and future collaborative training.

REFERENCES

Belet, M. (2018). Reducing interethnic bias through real-life and literacy encounters: The interplay between face-to-face and vicarious contact in high school classrooms. *Intercultural Journal of Intercultural Relations, 63*, 53–67.

Boyer, E.L. (1972, February 14). We must find new forms for higher education. *The Chronicle of Higher Education.* Retrieved at https://www.chronicle.com/article/we-must-find-new-forms-for-higher-education/

Collymore, K.V. (2020, July 1). Colleges must confront structural racism. *The Chronicle of Higher Education.* Retrieved at https://www.chronicle.com/article/colleges-must-confront-structural-racism?cid=gen_sign_in

Ezarik, M. (2021, May 6). More discussion than action: Racial justice on campus. *Inside Higher Ed.* Retrieved at https://www.insidehighered.com/news/2021/05/06/what-students-think-about-racial-justice-efforts-campus

Gallagher, S., & Palmer, J. (2020). The pandemic pushed universities online: The change was long overdue. *Harvard Business Review.* Retrieved at https://hbr.org/2020/09/the-pandemic-pushed-universities-online-the-change-was-long-overdue

García, E., & Weiss, E. (2020, September 10). COVID-19 and student performance, equity, and U.S. education policy: Lessons from pre-pandemic research to inform relief, recovery, and rebuilding. *Economic Policy Institute.* Retrieved at https://www.epi.org/publication/the-consequences-of-the-covid-19-pandemic-for-education-performance-and-equity-in-the-united-states-what-can-we-learn-from-pre-pandemic-research-to-inform-relief-recovery-and-rebuilding/

Govindarajan, V., & Srivastava, A. (2020, June 2). A post-pandemic strategy for U.S. higher ed. *Harvard Business Review.* Retrieved at https://hbr.org/2020/06/a-post-pandemic-strategy-for-u-s-higher-ed

Griffith, J.C. (2006). Transition from faculty to administrator and transition back to the faculty. *New Directions for Higher Education, 2006*(134), 67–77.

Gupta, S. (Host). (2020, June 8). The future of higher education. [Audio podcast episode]. In *Coronavirus: Fact vs. Fiction.* CNN Health. Retrieved at https://www.cnn.com/2020/06/08/health/gupta-coronavirus-podcast-wellness-june-8/index.html

Hess, A.J. (2018, August 30). Harvard Business School professor: Half of American colleges will be bankrupt in 10 to 15 years. *CNBC Make It.* Retrieved at https://www.cnbc.com/2018/08/30/hbs-prof-says-half-of-us-colleges-will-be-bankrupt-in-10-to-15-years.html

Koenig, R. (2019, December 11). Most students and faculty prefer face-to-face instruction, EDUCAUSE surveys find. *Digital Learning in Higher Ed.* Retrieved at https://www.edsurge.com/news/2019-12-11-most-students-and-faculty-prefer-face-to-face-instruction-educause-surveys-find

Lederman, D. (2017, April 28). Clay Christensen, Doubling Down. *Inside Higher Education.* Retrieved at https://www.insidehighered.com/digital-learning/article/2017/04/28/clay-christensen-sticks-predictions-massive-college-closures

Long, B.T. (2012). The financial crisis and college enrollment: How have students and their families responded? In J.R. Brown & C.M. Hoxby (Eds.), *How the financial crisis and great recession affected higher education.* University of Chicago Press.

Rapanta, C., Botturri, L, Goodyear, P., Guàrdia, L., & Koole, M. (2020). Online university teaching during and after the Covid-19 crisis: Refocusing teacher presence and learning activity. *Postdigital Science and Education, 2,* 923–945.

Roper, L.D. (2019). The power of dialogue and conversation in higher education. *New Directions for Student Leadership, 163,* 15–28.

Rosowsky, D., & Hallman, K. (2020, May 26). Communicating culture in a distributed world. *Inside Higher Ed.* Retrieved at https://www.insidehighered.com/views/2020/05/26/importance-culture-binding-higher-ed-institution-together-during-crises-pandemic

Simon, C. (2017, September 5). Bureaucrats and buildings: The case for why college is so expensive. *Forbes.* https://www.forbes.com/sites/carolinesimon/2017/09/05/bureaucrats-and-buildings-the-case-for-why-college-is-so-expensive/?sh=69439f68456a

Sulé, V.T. (2011). Restructuring the master's tools: Black female and Latina faculty navigating and contributing in classrooms through oppositional positions. *Equity and Excellence in Education, 44*(2), 169–187.

Tatum, B.D. (2019). The challenge of talking about racism on campus. *Daedalus, the Journal of the American Academy of Arts & Sciences, 148*(4), 79–93.

Whillans, A., Giurge, L.M., Macchia, L., & Yemiscigil, A. (2020, August 3). Why a Covid-19 world feels both tiring and hopeful for college students. *Harvard Business Review.* Retrieved at https://hbr.org/2020/08/why-a-covid-19-world-feels-both-tiring-and-hopeful-for-college-students

Chapter Four

Why Us? An Administrator and Faculty Member Join Forces

The premise of this book is that the relationships between administration and faculty are a cultural exchange, and that the predictable tensions between the two cultures can be reduced – and trust increased – when intercultural communication skills are practiced.

Dr. Helen Spencer-Oatey, whose professional/research experience combines the psychology and linguistics disciplines, founded the first graduate program in Intercultural Communication in the United Kingdom. She notes:

> Harmonious interpersonal relations are vitally important for individuals, social groupings, and whole nations. They are never easy to achieve but can be particularly challenging in intercultural contexts. They are therefore an extremely important facet of intercultural competence, yet strangely there has been little unpacking of what this means both conceptually and practically.
>
> (Spencer-Oatey, 2020, p. 13)

It is no wonder that Spencer-Oatey's work resonates with the authors of this book, as we also have roots in the field of psychology. Throughout our decades of professional work in higher education settings, we have drawn upon knowledge of psychology theory (clinical and developmental–educational) as we have navigated our respective roles and responsibilities. We are comfortable with applying some of the theory to our professional work-lives, and we have sometimes done so instinctively, as the lessons that are learned over decades of practice include seemingly simple skills such as: listening, observation, and empathy. While there are some conflicts that are not simple to confront and work through, being sensitive to human behavior – particularly behavior that results from trauma – has made us attuned to opportunities for connection and relationship-building.

DOI: 10.4324/9781003148739-5

LIFE IN THE TRENCHES

The expression "in the trenches" exemplifies quite literally the intercultural communication that occurred during World War I, "particularly in the close bonds between public-school-educated junior officers and the men, and the mixing of men from different areas after the introduction of conscription in 1916" (Walker, 2014, par. 3). The structure of the U.S. army on the front lines afforded soldiers time and opportunities for emotional bonding, and exchange of language and ideas that transformed all of them and the society that has followed over several generations.

Similarly, administrators and faculty members working in stressful conditions may refer to their own work "in the trenches," conjuring up associations with battles and wounds they've experienced on their own home fronts. Other researchers note the "dark side of academia" (Cantrell, 2016, p. 143) that is predictable when faculty become administrators. In an article by Gallos (2008), the author centers the analogy of the trenches, extending it even further by describing the toxicity of the trenches:

> [D]ealing over time with others' frustration, anger, and disappointment resulting from organizational life in a competitive world of scarce resources and nonstop change – can be hazardous to body and soul. It exaggerates feelings of managerial overload, diminishes creativity, and makes it harder to resolve everyday dilemmas. It can lull those exposed to the workplace affect into a complacency that keeps people and organizations locked in patterns that are productive for neither – and that block the development of structures and strategies for a healthy workplace.
>
> (p. 354)

The author proposes a new role for organizations and workplaces: "organizational toxin handler." Gallos (2008) suggests that organizations are social systems and therefore are composed of people "who respond with a range of emotions to the challenges, disruptions, and demands experienced every day at work" (p. 355). People – not necessarily tied to any hierarchical job structure – in positions where their primary responsibility is to "facilitate open communications, conflict resolution, and understanding among diverse individuals" can contribute to the evolution of "compassionate cultures and collaborative efforts that benefit multiple stakeholders" (p. 355). Over time, and with a track record that includes tangible successes (small and large), an institutional community can develop trusting relationships and therefore a strong foundation that will support the community during challenging times and stress.

As you read the examples below, see if you recognize someone – perhaps yourself – in your current workplace who embodies these actions/roles:

- a colleague who is routinely sought out as a sounding board for people's venting and complaining and in return shares potential strategies and empathy
- a colleague who proactively offers suggestions that help others avoid tense or generally unpleasant interactions with a supervisor
- a colleague who picks up the slack when others do not complete their work for a host of reasons, personal and/or professional
- a colleague who invites others to occasional social gatherings (e.g., lunches, evening drinks, apple-picking expeditions) to build relationships outside of work

There is a tendency in institutions of higher education for patterns to form and people who make the effort to engage colleagues in soul-strengthening interactions to be highly valued members of the community. These efforts ultimately contribute to productivity and sustainability in the workplace and demonstrate informal leadership skills within administrator and faculty cultures.

ONE SIZE DOES NOT FIT ALL

With regard to leadership and academic institutions, experts recognize that so-called "best practices" are well-intended but are not always a fit for every institution, "because each organization has its own values, norms, practices, and cultures" (Siu, 2021, p. 25). A cultural approach differs from an organizational approach that emphasizes change guided by leaders who fit a desired ideal or mold that is firmly established at the highest level of authority. A cultural approach "considers what leaders and managers have or have not said or done that creates social messages for employees" (p. 23). Such messages can include confusing norms around hiring faculty and staff, strategic plans and vision statements, and what gets accomplished and what is left in institutional limbo due to increasing layers of administrative vetting. As the authors of this book, we recognize our own positionality that contributed to the experiences and relationships that scaffolded the research for this book. Rather than share best practices, the sections that follow invite consideration of our own cultural and intercultural experiences.

The Consummate Other

Whether by choice or circumstance, women in various positions in higher education are in a complicated position of the "other." Women continue to be paid less than male counterparts, with reports estimating an 11% salary differential between female and male faculty members (Zalaznick, 2020) and statistics noting that while 60% of all higher education professionals are women, 82% of "number one earners are men. And women of color are 'virtually nonexistent' among the top earning positions in higher education" (Arnett, 2021, par. 1).

Throughout our own professional experiences, we have participated in workplace conversations and investigations into salary gaps, as well as conversations about how women behave (or should behave, or are perceived to behave) in their respective roles in higher education. These themes are prevalent in research literature.

Some researchers note that women – especially women leaders – "may suffer from the 'double-bind' because women who emphasize competition and instrumentality may be judged too agentic yet women who emphasize group processes and consensus may be judged too communal" (Brower, Schwartz, & Jones, 2019, p. 121). When researchers consider cultural characteristics of women in higher education contexts, findings often note a collective impulse that guides women's leadership, such as: "Women are more likely to make decisions out of concern for specific individuals and within the context of the situation. Women, therefore, value connectedness and relationships" (Ballenger, 2010, p. 5).

While there has been progress made in the number of women represented in the highest level of university leadership, statistics indicate a recent slowing of such progress:

> Only 30.1 percent of presidencies were held by women in 2016, up from 26.4 percent in 2011 and 23 percent in 2006. The rate of increase has slowed considerably in recent years – it grew from 9.5 percent in 1986 to 21.1 percent in 2001.
>
> (Seltzer, 2017, par. 7)

Further complicating generalizations stemming from data collection, public institutions recently feature a higher percentage of women presidents than private nonprofit institutions, and public institutions of higher education are more likely to have a minority president than private institutions (public = 22.3% and private = 10.6% in 2016) (American Council on Education, 2017). While there is no one explanation as to why women and men experience the realities reflected in the data, as long as organizational systems represent the larger society and political climate in which they reside (Bartels et al., 2021), then it is imperative that structural systems change to represent a more equitable society.

Some concrete first steps that institutions of higher education can take to shift the numbers in a more equitable, diverse direction are to examine existing diversity, equity, inclusion, and justice policies and plans. Researchers note that in addition to evaluating the effectiveness of these policies and plans, any efforts to establish an authentic, diverse female faculty and administrative employee pool must be paired with "structured mentoring activities and professional development programs" that will help women who aspire to upper-level administrative leadership (Ballenger, 2010, p. 17). As mentioned previously in this book, checking off items on a checklist does not lead to meaningful, sustainable change. In order to invest in such deep and responsive change, we argue that it is vital to develop intercultural skills that are more than perfunctory or performative.

Awareness, Competence, and Communication

Research literature delineates between surface-level understanding of terms (awareness), and related behaviors manifest in society, and deeper, more transformative understanding of difference that impacts how humans interact with each other. Much about cultural interactions can be found in research related to the medical profession (e.g., Tervalon & Murray-García, 1997), and many researchers emphasize cultural proficiency in order to improve business practices (e.g., Nongard, 2018). Some universities define intercultural competence so they can teach, assess, and measure desired outcomes in their students. Any university with an International Relations program or intercultural programs and courses has likely attempted to clarify and define what they value and how that is being taught, and whether or not they've been successful. Some guiding questions that help facilitate reflection and discussion about this type of work in higher education include:

1. What is "successful" intercultural communication?
2. What skills do we need to develop in order to be successful?

Higher education administrators and faculty members have spent many years in pursuit of answers to these questions. In preparation for the writing of this book, we engaged in our own research and conversations with colleagues – grounding our research in the work and words of experts in intercultural communication. We present some of our most impactful learning in the sections that follow, and then we will transition into Part

Two of this book to provide readers with a deeper understanding of the cultural priorities for administrators and faculty members.

INTERCULTURAL (R)EVOLUTION IN THEORY

We have mentioned scholars in the field of intercultural communication throughout this book. Within the academic literature, many experts cite Deardorff (2006) as among the first to seek out and document consensus among intercultural scholars and academic administrators about what constitutes intercultural competence and the best ways to measure it. In one study conducted with administrators at 24 institutions across the United States, representing a range of institutions from community colleges through large research universities, she achieved consensus on some elements and principles that rest under the intercultural umbrella.

The definition deemed most applicable to institutions' internationalization (a.k.a., globalization) strategies was one derived from Byram's (1997) work on intercultural competence: "Knowledge of others; knowledge of self; skills to interpret and relate; skills to discover and/or to interact; valuing others' values, beliefs, and behaviors; and relativizing one's self" (Byram, 1997, p. 34). For more than the past decade, researchers have moved beyond competence framed in a globalization initiative to a deeply held institutional goal of communicating within and across cultures. For example, some researchers (e.g., Debray & Spencer-Oatey, 2019) have examined patterns of participation and positionality, noting how experiences over time contribute to the silencing and marginalization of individuals within group contexts. Some institutions have developed their own definitions over time, specifically tied to their institutional context. The topics many institutions speak to most often include active perception and processing:

- increasing awareness of cultural groups and belonging
- reflecting upon how different cultural groups are valued in a given setting
- understanding cultural differences by experiencing other cultures
- actively reflecting to deepen self-awareness of one's own culture

These elements and actions move beyond the starting point – the importance of cultural awareness and the ability to demonstrate competence. Scholars resonate with the notion of reaching a critical, transformative point: "[t]he ability to communicate effectively and appropriately in intercultural situations based on one's intercultural knowledge, skills, and attitudes" (Deardorff, 2004, p. 194).

According to Deardorff (2006), specific important intercultural communication skills are consistently agreed upon by research participants, which include skills to listen and observe, as well as to analyze, interpret, and relate to others. These are skills that we noted at the beginning of this chapter, which we feel have been critical to our own developing repertoire for interacting with colleagues in higher education settings. As the field of intercultural communication continues to develop and evolve, more recent research grounded in "historical, institutional, and/or methodological encounters" (Rampton, Maybin, & Roberts, 2015, p. 14) affirms the utility of such skills when communicating with people of different cultural groups. In a higher education setting, community members' attitudes related to openness, respect for others as evident in words and actions, and a tolerance for ambiguity are critical for successful intercultural communication.

Examples reported in the research literature, similar to ones you have likely experienced in many academic disagreements or tense intercultural interactions, demonstrate that it is easy for members of one cultural group to judge the other based on their own cultural understandings or norms. It takes effort to approach a situation with an attitude of discovery – a disposition toward tolerating ambiguity – with the flexibility of mind and spirit required to truly understand someone else's worldview.

CULTURAL NORMS

The word "norms" is considered in one of two ways in the field of intercultural communication – descriptive norms and injunctive norms. Descriptive norms refer to "what is typically/usually said or done" and injunctive norms refer to "what people believe ought to be said or done, or what ought to be avoided" (Spencer-Oatey, 2020, p. 7). In higher education settings, as well as most interpersonal interactions, injunctive norms are viewed as having greater potential impact on trust and rapport if these types of norms are violated. It's critically important to recognize, however, that the context for existing norms varies from setting to setting, so what is an acceptable cultural norm in one institution may not be acceptable in another institution. Spencer-Oatey (2020) raises a point related to intercultural competence:

> [H]ow feasible is it for anyone to understand the cultural norms for all social groups and in all contexts? I would argue that this is an impossible task for anyone. The goal should not be for people to understand (in advance) what norms will be operating in innumerable unspecified situations, but rather to have the ability to perceive norms, whatever context they find themselves in.
>
> (p. 7)

What would happen if administrators and faculty members turned their focus toward questions that would bring these cultural groups closer, toward shared goals? Employees in workplaces are "comfortable with ambition, competition and success...[yet] the questions of how we value relationships and, in particular, how far we value being true and being helpful to others" (Leung, 2008, pp. 165–166) is less familiar.

Comfort in Conflict

Leung (2008) argues that culture and how it affects conflict-resolution are vital in any effort to study conflict in the workplace. She notes the often-noted "individualism-collectivism" dynamic, where some cultures (e.g., Western cultures) place emphasis on individual wants and needs and value privacy and personal space, whereas other cultures (e.g., Asian cultures) prioritize conflict avoidance and value harmony and conformity. Challenges arise in higher education settings when administrators and faculty members, most associated with individual and collective cultures, respectively by virtue of their roles and responsibilities, attempt to resolve conflicts – even proactively. The cultural dynamics that these two groups revert to reflexively, whether due to bias or habit, sometimes impede successful intercultural communication.

> [P]eople may be able to build up their understanding of norms in given contexts with certain types of participants. However, it must always be remembered that if the participants change (e.g., university academics rather than government officials, even when the nationalities are kept constant) and/or if the communicative activity changes, the norms and associated expectations will change too.
> (Spencer-Oatey, 2020, p. 8)

As the authors of this book joined forces over time, to investigate conflict and share perspectives, we found examples of successful intercultural communication that informed our work in our respective workplace environments.

INTERCULTURAL (R)EVOLUTION IN PRACTICE

There is a consistent question that has been implied or explicitly stated in intercultural communication literature: "[W]hat happens when discourse norms are different, but there is an intention to reach an understanding?" (Fox, 1997, p. 86). Individuals and groups, representing administrators and faculty scholars, have delved into this question for many years. At the University of Warwick, the GlobalPeople initiative aims to strengthen people's practice and comfort with intercultural communication along a continuum of practice. Dr. Helen Spencer-Oatey (2020) refers to the work as "global fitness":

> [In] order to foster intercultural competence, people need to move outside of their comfort zones and face up to the disorienting encounters that inevitably arise when moving into unfamiliar situations. Importantly, though, this is not enough on its own; people also need to manage their emotions, reflect on their experiences, thinking them through from different perspectives, and then making behavioural adjustments. In other words, they need to mindfully reflect and stretch.
>
> (p. 8)

Table 4.1 illustrates the growth strategies that build intercultural skills according to Spencer-Oatey's concept of global fitness.

As people gain experience feeling comfortable with disequilibrium that can arise in unfamiliar territory, they gain strengths that contribute to their institutional wellbeing. The premise of a continuum has been articulated in a model that has, not surprisingly, been adopted into the curriculum of many higher education business programs. The elements highlighted in the stages of the continuum can be applied across many settings.

Intercultural Development Continuum

The Intercultural Development Inventory® (IDI®) "is used by thousands of individuals and organizations to build intercultural competence to achieve international and domestic diversity and inclusion goals and outcomes"

Table 4.1 Developing Global Fitness

Strategies for growth	Build global fitness
Leave comfort zone	Intercultural vitality
Engage with difference	Intercultural understanding
Mindfully reflect and stretch	Intercultural skillfulness in communication
Consult others/seek support	Intercultural skillfulness in relating
Manage stress	

Adapted from Spencer-Oatey, H. (2020). Intercultural competence and harmonious intercultural relations: Interdisciplinary perspectives and insights. *China Media Research, 16*(2), 1–13.

(Hammer, 2021, par. 1). The IDI® is an assessment tool for organizations to use as a way of getting a sense of an organization's capacity to interact meaningfully with members of different cultures and organizations. Fundamental to the model are a measurable set of skills, attitudes, and knowledge that contribute to the capacity of an organization, and its community members, to demonstrate intercultural competence and communication. The underlying assumption is that a baseline measure of an institution can be attained, and then, with practice and intention, people can gain skills that translate into improved relationships and greater awareness of cultural difference, as well as connections that enhance the health of the institution. As an organization develops knowledge and skills that move them as a collective whole from a "monocultural" to an "intercultural" mindset, there are stages of development that are evident: denial, polarization, minimization, acceptance, and adaptation.

Denial

Individuals who demonstrate a "denial" mindset typically display disinterest in cultures other than their own and avoidance of difference as much as possible. People who have little experience interacting with members of other cultural groups resort to what they think they know, based on generalizations or stereotypes about the other groups. It is typical for people who are somewhat isolated from larger, more diverse communities to have this perspective, and they tend to discount cultural diversity to instead tune into their own feelings/associations or what they perceive through their lenses to be the norm.

Polarization

Polarization, while farther along the continuum in a positive direction, includes more conflict and negative energy. This so-called "us vs. them" perception of culture exists in the workplace and is all too common in higher education communities. People at this level tend to evaluate their institutions and make judgments at the extremes, either from a defensive stance where an individual thinks their culture is better than others, or when they think the opposite, that other cultures are all better than their own. Diversity in institutions that score high in this category tend to experience diversity as "uncomfortable."

Minimization

This stage along the continuum is considered a transitional point, as this stage highlights what is similar between groups and some universal values and guiding beliefs held among groups. Many people working in institutions where this perspective is common note that diversity is often met with a lack of deep listening that translates into visible actions. Emphasizing how people are all similar doesn't allow space for difference to exist and be respected. As one component among many co-existing entities noted in the continuum, there are distinguishable cultures that exist (Hammer, 2021). Self-reflection is a skill encouraged throughout the exploration process.

Acceptance

People and organizations that have reached this stage are situated in the intercultural/global mindset along the Intercultural continuum. People are able to recognize and respect cultural differences and similarities within their own culture. Diversity feels "understood" at this stage, but people (whose responses put them in this category) sometimes project their cultural understanding about some groups onto someone else. People at this stage often do not progress any farther along the continuum.

Adaptation

People who are at this stage along the continuum are often able to shift their own perspective about cultural groups and also shift their behavior, accordingly. Diversity is experienced by community members as being valued and exemplified in the institution, according to the IDI® categories. Some people at this stage, however, can be frustrated with others who work with cultural differences from a different orientation.

For most of the people who have worked with this tool, the best takeaway was the increased intercultural sensitivity demonstrated within the institution. Some people find that they alter their beliefs and practices as a result of the process, and some instead affirm their previously held beliefs and practices. Regardless of the outcome, the process results in opportunities for community members to interact, form relationships, and learn from and with each other.

THE JOURNEY BEGINS AT HOME

The overarching goal and motivation for writing this book is for us to share resources with others so that administrators and faculty members can learn and adapt as appropriate within their own specific contexts. We expect that the tools and collective practice will contribute to the necessary skills for successful intercultural communication. Stated simply, our mission is to help you cultivate the capacity to understand the perspective of the other. Every word in that statement matters:

- **Cultivate** – This requires action, practice, and care.
- **Capacity** – This includes (1) awareness of different perspectives and/or culture and of your own perspective and/or culture; and (2) the ability to practice cognitive flexibility and to tolerate ambiguity.
- **Understand the perspective of the other** – This includes consideration of another person's worldview and practicing empathy.

Figure 4.1 illustrates these ideas and how they build upon each other.

Throughout the following chapters, we'll explore what it looks like to put these principles to use, using actual scenarios that may feel eerily familiar to anyone working within a higher education setting. These scenarios are based on the lived experiences of many people whose stories shared many common themes and plot points. We'll explore administration and faculty as two different cultures and address some of the common themes that often contribute to tension in the institution.

Then, we'll walk through the steps that constitute a practice to help you cultivate the capacity to understand the perspective of the other. We encourage you to explore these scenarios, the practice and reflection questions in each chapter, and the additional resources on your own *and* with a group of colleagues. We have found it useful for people to practice understanding the perspective of another in non-threatening situations, when

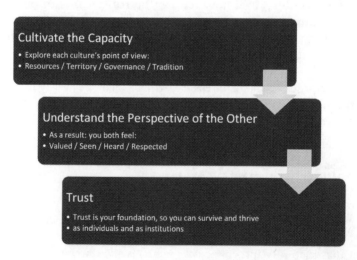

Figure 4.1 Cultivating the capacity to understand the perspective of the other.

the stakes are low. That way, you build skills and reflexes so that you're able to draw upon the same skills when the stakes are high.

As you practice processing low-stakes situations in hypothetical discussions or in real-life situations, you will begin to realize that your perspective of the other person's motives or opinions is often just a story you've been telling yourself about that other person and their thinking, their motives, and what validates their actions. As you practice asking questions, you gain new, increased awareness of the other person or group. Once you build your tolerance for ambiguity, your attitude changes to one of curiosity and discovery, and in that mindset, you are more open to learning and understanding the other worldview. You might find you have something in common after all.

PREPARING FOR THE JOURNEY

We have already addressed the uncertainty facing many institutions of higher education in the immediate, post-COVID landscape. The violent, tragic murder of George Floyd and too many other Black individuals at the hands of police, and the antiracist movements that have grown across the United States, have already spurred many higher education communities to seek out resources to help them understand cultures and perspectives different from their own. If "[s]ystems are representative of the larger society and political climate in which they reside," (Bartels et al., 2021) then institutions of higher education have much work ahead of them to develop collaborative, respectful campus communities. Those invested in the work advocate for "structures and strategies that promote caring cultures, individual resiliency, *and* extraordinary performance: models that support high productivity *and* high attention to human needs at work" (Gallos, 2008, p. 364). People are ready to listen and learn, and people want to work in an academic community with which they are proud to identify.

SUMMARY

Administrators and faculty members experience predictable tensions in higher education, and the authors have spent years conducting and analyzing research, as well as learning from their professional workplace experiences. Calling upon the work that exists in the evolving field of intercultural communication, people can practice skills as they acquire knowledge and skills that contribute to more successful and harmonious workplace environments. When administrators and faculty join forces, their combined efforts result in more productive, healthier institutions.

PRACTICE AND REFLECTION

1. Consider a time when you have acted, or hesitated to act, in a way that could be perceived by others as "difficult." What were the reactions of others, and how did those actions make you feel? Describe whether you sought alternative feedback to validate what you were told, or whether you felt shut down, and what steps you took either way to process your thoughts and feelings.
2. Describe a committee or task force in your workplace that features administrators and faculty members. How is power distributed? How are agendas set and/or votes taken? What happens when there are differences of opinion among members?
3. As you consider groups that exist in your institution related to diversity (e.g., Diversity Council, DEI task force, affinity groups), what are the practices for people to communicate within and across these groups? How are decisions made about communicating throughout the workplace community, supporting specific initiatives, and/or promoting some or all perspectives? Where is there room for improvement, and what would it take to make some positive progress?

RESOURCES

Dragon Boat Festival

https://publicholidays.cn/dragon-boat-festival/

The Dragon Boat Festival is celebrated in mainland China, as well as Hong Kong, Macau, and in cities in countries around the world. The event features dance performances, food markets and stalls, and the primary focus – competitive races between teams of paddlers and drummers. This type of team event was very successful in building community among administrators, faculty, staff, and community members from the university and people who had traveled from all over the world to participate in the event's festivities.

NCAA Annual Conference

https://www.ncaa.org/about/resources/events/convention

This annual convention attracts representatives from institutions of higher education who have roles in academic institutions that range from the students to the upper administration. These events provide an opportunity for members of academic communities to mingle and share conversations and decision-making around topics of shared importance. One doesn't have to have a vested interest in athletics to participate in a meaningful and satisfying way. Keeping students' interests and wellbeing at the core of the work provides a level playing field in ways not often experienced in other conventions for academic personnel.

Mothers in Academia

https://www.amazon.com/Mothers-Academia-Mari-Castaneda/dp/0231160054/ref=sr_1_18?dchild=1&keywords=women+in+academia+book&qid=1623004379&sr=8-18

This book, written by authors Maria Castaneda and Kirsten Isgro, is one that specifically addresses challenges faced by women in higher education who are also mothers, balancing numerous priorities in their work and home lives. This book serves as a wonderful book group read or pre-read in advance of a working group dedicated to work–life balance. We recommend inviting members of the university with roles different from each other – faculty and administrators, primarily – to use this opportunity to read, reflect, and notice what resonates with them and what motivates them to enact change in their own environments.

REFERENCES

American Council on Education. (2017). *American College President study*. Retrieved at https://www.aceacps.org/summary-profile/

Arnett, A.A. (2021, February 24). Report examines gender pay disparities among top earners in higher ed. *Diverse Issues in Higher Education*. Retrieved at https://diverseeducation.com/article/206316/

Ballenger, J. (2010). Women's access to higher education leadership: Cultural and structural barriers. *Forum on Public Policy Online*, 5, 1–20.

Bartels, L.K., Weissinger, S.E., O'Brien, L.C., Ball, J.C., Cobb, P.D., Harris, J., Morgan, S.M., Love, E., Moody, S.B., & Feldmann, M.L. (2021, January). Developing a system to support the advancement of women in higher education. *The Journal of Faculty Development*, 35(1), 34–42.

Brower, R.L., Schwartz, R.A., & Jones, T.B. (2019). "Is it because I'm a woman?" Gender-based attributional ambiguity in higher education administration. *Gender and Education*, 31(1), 117–135.

Byram, M. (1997). *Teaching and Assessing Intercultural Communicative competence*. Retrieved at https://www.google.com/books/edition/Teaching_and_Assessing_Intercultural_Com/0vfq8JJWhTsC?hl=en&gbpv=1&printsec=frontcover

Cantrell, P. (2016). Leadership in academia: *Dean's Disease* – Its sources, seductions, and solutions. *Journal of Values-Based Leadership*, 9(2), 143–149.

Deardorff, D.K. (2004). *The identification and assessment of intercultural competence as a student outcome of international education at institutions of higher education in the United States.* North Carolina State University.

Deardorff, D.K. (2006). Identification and assessment of intercultural competence as a student outcome of internalization. *Journal of Studies in International Education, 10*(3), 241–266.

Debray, C., & Spencer-Oatey, H. (2019). "On the same page?" Marginalisation and positioning practices in intercultural teams. *Journal of Pragmatics, 144,* 15–28.

Fox, C. (1997). The authenticity of intercultural communication. *International Journal of Intercultural Relations, 21*(1), 85–103.

Gallos, J.V. (2008 December). Learning from the toxic trenches: The winding road to healthier organizations – and to healthy everyday leaders. *Journal of Management Inquiry, 17*(4), 354–367.

Hammer, M.R. (2021). The roadmap to intercultural competence using the IDI. *IDI, LLC.* Retrieved at https://idiinventory.com/generalinformation/

Leung, A.S.M. (2008). Interpersonal conflict and resolution strategies: An examination of Hong Kong employees. *Team Performance Management, 14*(3/4), 165–178.

Nongard, R. (2018, August 20). 6 ways businesses benefit from cultural competence. *Business.com.* Retrieved at https://www.business.com/articles/business-cultural-competence/

Rampton, B., Maybin, J., & Roberts, C. (2015). Theory and method in linguistic ethnography. In J. Snell et al. (Eds.), *Linguistic ethnography* (pp. 14–50). Palgrave Macmillan.

Seltzer, R. (2017, June 20). The slowly diversifying presidency. *Inside Higher Ed.* Retrieved at https://www.insidehighered.com/news/2017/06/20/college-presidents-diversifying-slowly-and-growing-older-study-finds

Siu, B. (2021). *Opening doors to diversity in leadership.* University of Toronto Press.

Spencer-Oatey, H. (2020). Intercultural competence and harmonious intercultural relations: Interdisciplinary perspectives and insights. *China Media Research, 16*(2), 1–13.

Tervalon, M., & Murray-García, J. (1998, May). Cultural humility versus cultural competence: A critical distinction in defining physician training outcomes in multicultural education. *Journal of Health Care for the Poor and Underserved, 9*(2), 117–125.

Walker, J. (2014, July 23). Trench talk: A guide to first world war slang. *The Guardian.* Retrieved at https://www.theguardian.com/education/2014/jul/23/first-world-war-slang-glossary

Zalaznick, M. (2020, November 2). Here's a snapshot of the gender pay gap in higher ed. *University Business.* Retrieved at https://universitybusiness.com/gender-pay-gap-persists-male-female-professors-higher-ed/

Part Two

Two Cultures Building Bridges

Chapter Five

Cultural Priority: Resources

Tensions exist between faculty and administrators in higher education. We know this to be true, and the tensions will likely continue to exist as long as these two cultural groups exist and are made up of human beings with human emotions, ideas, and priorities. Institutions of higher education haven't been around as long as human social groups have been recorded, but tensions and resulting conflicts that exist between social groups have been documented for thousands of years in written and oral history (see the digital collections in the Library of Congress for some wonderful examples of oral histories) and artistic representations (e.g., Pérez-Villanueva, 2021).

Beginning with this chapter, this part of our book presents cultural priorities that are shared by faculty and administrators, and which contribute to tensions in higher education. Looking at the priorities through an intercultural lens, we provide concrete examples that serve as case studies to explore. We also provide explicit perspectives of faculty and administrators, which are the result of our formal research study and decades of informal professional discourse with colleagues in workplace settings and academic conference venues. As mentioned previously in Chapter Two, while these case studies may seem very familiar, they are amalgams. We therefore borrow from the film industry and articulate our own "disclaimer" that "any similarities to persons living or dead, or actual events is purely coincidental."

RESOURCES UNDER THREAT

We begin with a focus on resources as a cultural priority – who has them, who wants them, who makes decisions about them, and more. Tensions over resources have been identified as one of the main reasons for war throughout history (Goodman, 2021). While tensions in higher education don't equate to war as most people define it, we are already familiar with expressions that stem from war-time parlance. These include experiences described by researchers and participants as being "in the trenches," or actions taken by faculty or administrators being "over the top." Goodman (2021) provides definitions of war that include a "state of competition or hostility between different people or groups" (par. 2). It is precisely this perception of hostility between faculty and administrator groups that conjures the sensation of being in battle – sometimes prolonged conflict.

One more analogy that is used across disciplines (e.g., political science, history, science, economics) and is applicable in this chapter, the "tragedy of the commons" provides some insights into the ways resources are valued, protected, and contested in higher education contexts. Spiliakos (2019) describes the tragedy of the commons as "a situation in which individuals with access to a shared resource (also called a common) act in their own interest and, in doing so, ultimately deplete the resource" (par. 4). The theory is anchored in economics, and original conceptualization has been attributed to British writer William Forster Lloyd in 1833 and made popular by Garrett Hardin in 1968. The relationship of this theory to resources in higher education is apt:

> This theory explains individuals' tendency to make the best decisions for their personal situation, regardless of the negative impact they may have on others. An individual's belief that others won't act in the best interest of the group can lead them to justify their selfish behavior. When facing the use or potential overuse of a common or public good, individuals may act with their short-term best interest in mind, for instance, using an unsustainable product, and disregard the harm it could cause to the environment or general public.
>
> (Spiliakos, 2019, par. 6)

Within this brief definition of the theory, we can point to concepts already presented in this book, such as the individual vs. collective styles of decision-making discussed in Chapter Four, and the notion of governance briefly presented in Chapter Two, which will be discussed in much greater detail in Chapter Seven. The other important factor to consider, which stems from the field of psychology, is the role of perception in human behavior. The description of the tragedy of the commons above notes that the "belief" that someone may act in a certain way is enough to prompt others to act in an attempt to preserve the resources that are perceived to be under threat. These perceptions of threat, whether real or imagined, can increase anxiety, reinforce suspicion and mistrust, and hinder effectiveness that contributes to a healthy institution. In the case study that follows, see what specific behaviors and/or communication (or the absence of these) contribute to the tensions that exist among faculty and administrators.

CULTURAL PRIORITY: RESOURCES

CASE STUDY: AN ACADEMIC PROGRAM IS CANCELLED

Brayton clenched and stretched his fingers into and out of fists as he walked toward the conference hall. His shirt collar felt tighter than it had when he'd dressed for work this morning, and he was glad that he was wearing a sports jacket so he didn't need to worry about sweat being visible to others. The hum of chatter in the hall rang in his ears as a familiar buzz – he estimated the room to be crowded with 50, maybe 60 faculty members. Ingrid, the chief academic officer, greeted him as he strode up the steps toward the conference hall.

"Ready for this one, Dean? I thought I'd wait so I could give you some cover," she said, grinning with closed lips as she rested her hand gently on the door handle. The two of them had been through difficult meetings together before and had bonded as a result of sharing war stories and comparing battle scars.

"Ready as I'll ever be," Brayton replied, noting how dry his mouth felt. Now, he wished he'd brought that water bottle with him. He'd decided against it because he didn't want to have to drink from it during the meeting, imagining that any indication of thirst would be perceived as a weakness, and he didn't want to encourage the hyenas to pounce.

As Ingrid held the door to the conference hall open, Brayton walked into the space and made a quick scan of the room, nodding his head in greeting as he made eye-contact with a few faculty members. He noticed that the chairs were arranged in a U-shape, presumably to imply "we're about to engage in community dialogue" as opposed to "you're about to be lectured at by your dean." He hoped the set-up would permeate some of the group's subconscious thinking and stave off unnecessary contention. He reached the podium and pulled the USB flash drive from his breast pocket, and he was grateful that he was able to insert it, without fumbling, into the laptop set up for the meeting. As soon as he opened the presentation on the big screen, the chatter in the room subsided as people started to notice that business was about to begin.

Brayton launched into his presentation, which featured his go-to format – one he borrowed from the chancellor he'd worked under at his previous institution. He started with quantitative statistics and updates: "…revenue and expenses…comparable institutions… matriculation shortfall…have to make some cuts…" He noticed the predictable glazed looks among some faculty faces, and the also predictable glares of other faculty members taking frantic notes. Then, he reached the slide that he knew would be the bomb, and he hesitated for a fraction of a second, hoping that he could avoid the inevitable clearing of his throat reflex that he often experienced when he felt uncomfortable delivering news to a group. His mind darted to a time when he had to tell his mom that he couldn't make it home for Thanksgiving, but then he quickly focused and said in what he hoped was a calm, authoritative voice, "A decision had to be made to cancel the archaeology program."

"We've gone to great lengths to prevent this, but it needs to happen. As you know, umm...we've had numerous meetings and discussions about it, and umm...looked at different ways to remediate the program to avoid closing it. But enrollments are just too small for us to umm...justify continuing this program at this time. All students currently in the program will be taken care of, and we're already creating short- and longer-term pathways for them to complete their required coursework. Are there any questions?" Brayton paused, feeling like he'd just talked *way* too fast. He really wished he had some water.

From his perch at the front, Brayton stared out at a room full of eyes either giving him icy stares or looking down at their cellphones. "Wonder what they're typing about?" he thought wryly. A ripple of sound began snaking its way across the room: murmurs between faculty members, fingers typing on keyboards or texting, people clearing their throats while shooting glances back and forth to each other. He asked again, "Are there any questions?"

Arlene, a faculty member in the Anthropology Department that included the archaeology program, raised her hand and began speaking simultaneously,

> I noticed that you used the passive voice? You said, 'a decision had to be made,' and I can't help but think that this puts safe distance between you and the final decision. If you didn't make the decision, who made the decision?

A moment of awkward silence filled the room, and Brayton responded quickly to fill the gap.

"Of course this is regrettable, but in these times of shrinking budgets and declining enrollments, at the end of the day we are simply not able to continue this program. We've already communicated this to the Board in our meeting just yesterday. Of course, we'll take care of the students, and I know I can count on you to rise to the occasion." There was a titter in the back of the room, and a few faculty smiled and looked down, trying not to laugh. "God, that's rude," Brayton thought before continuing.

"We are in unprecedented budgetary times. We have to devote our resources to programs thoughtfully and strategically. These decisions align with our strategic plan, and we've had a very transparent strategic planning process. But I am here to be very transparent with you, and I am available to answer any questions you have."

A few faculty members asked benign questions in the time that followed, and Ingrid looked at him, nodding approvingly throughout the meeting. When the meeting concluded, most people exited the room quickly and quietly. Brayton decided to take the long way back to his office so that he could walk and practice some of the Navy Seal breathing techniques he'd recently read about – he wanted to stay sharp.

FACULTY MEMBER K'S PERSPECTIVE

What follows is the reaction of a composite faculty member, created by integrating reactions from focus group participants, survey respondents, and conversations with professional colleagues in higher education settings.

"It's all bulls***."

"All the talk about the strategic plan—the Board eats it up, but it never lands well with the faculty. There's never an implementation plan. They're giving us this strategic plan but there is never any actual budget or implementation plan for how to get the resources to put these ideas into action."

"As for the announcement about canceling the program, it's news to everyone. It feels like a death. They're killing something that people have built. Some of the courses may still live on, but the program itself won't. You know that GIF of someone walking away from a car that explodes in the background? That's what I was picturing the whole time – Brayton the dean, striding confidently away from his car and, still walking, and raising his fist, holding the detonator up toward the sky…KABOOM! How can they do this? No one told us. What strategic plan? We had no say in this."

"I can't quite explain it, but you feel like you've fallen asleep and missed something. You feel like that deer in the headlights. How did this happen again? I think he purposely shows us statistics and numbers at the beginning so that we're lulled into submission."

"Then the dean keeps asking if we have any questions, but we're all in shock! The questions won't arise until we've processed the news, and then what? Some faculty had to leave the meeting and hurry to get to teach their next class, so people didn't have the time to process the news in that moment. But rest assured, after a few days we'll be mad as hell."

"We'll probably meet up with other faculty members in the café and start to ponder and exchange theories. There will be questions like, 'What does this mean for our jobs and our workload?' and 'What does this mean for everything we've built?' People don't want to let something die. We don't want a beloved program to vanish from the face of the earth, cuz then what happens to the field in general?

"You watch – some people have already started to strategize: which board members should we contact? Who wants to start writing the petition? We should let students know so they can decide to contact people or organize some sort of action."

ADMINISTRATOR S'S PERSPECTIVE

What follows is the reaction of a composite administrator, created by integrating reactions from focus group participants, survey respondents, and conversations with professional colleagues in higher education settings.

"After a meeting like that, and the negative reactions that will, *no doubt,* ensue from frustrated faculty, administrators want to go grab some beers and talk about the faculty. But they rarely do – number 1, because they're already on to the next thing, and number 2, because they're not close enough or don't feel safe enough with administrative colleagues to share how they really feel. They'd need to find a secluded place in another country to be able to speak freely."

"Faculty just don't get it. They're in their own ivory tower. They don't understand. What is wrong with them? Do they not read our emails? Do they not remember? We've sent out notifications, we've followed all the policies. We're doing everything we can to save this institution. Don't they get that?"

"When I was a dean, my administrators were pushing me to shut down a program. First I tried to fix it by warning the faculty that it was in trouble and giving them a year to attract more students. But they didn't do anything about it. So I had to announce: *we have to teach out this program.* I didn't want to shut it down. I was extremely disappointed about it, but at that point we had no other choice. Some faculty and I ended up having a wake for it in my office."

"It was after that point that some faculty members finally came to me with new ideas, ready to make some compromises to save the program: 'What if we do X, Y and Z? Then can we keep it?' I really did believe in that program and wanted to be able to help them save it. They persuaded me, and I changed my decision and fought for it, which meant I had to put myself on the line and convince several upper-level administrators to let me keep it. It was only saved because both sides ultimately listened to each other and worked out a solution."

How can compromises or collaborative problem-solving become more common in higher education contexts? In the following sections, we explore cultural elements that can inform your own consideration of resources and decision-making in your own setting.

CULTURAL CONTEXT

There are important, valid reasons for faculty members to respond angrily and/or defensively after being told a program will be canceled. While there are rules that inform and guide the process of canceling and "teaching out" a program, these guidelines don't often rise to the level of awareness for faculty members who are primarily concerned with ensuring that current students in the pipeline can complete their degree at the university or transfer to a comparable school within the same geographic area or with a similar program. As with rules of engagement that guide military activities, rules that guide program cancellations feel more like a courtesy from days of yore than a useful strategy when trust is lacking and the administration is perceived as the enemy.

Students' Concerns

Similarly, current students, as well as alumni of the program, can suffer a real loss of faith in their institution – typically linked with announcements made by administrators – and they often question the value of their degree if they know the program will cease to exist in the near future. Outraged alumni have been known to publicly push back against program and institution closures (Whitford, 2020; Zheng, 2019), and many staff and faculty begin (if they hadn't already) to lose hope in their own futures at the institution. Even if students are able to complete their programs with integrity, they understandably wonder if they will have an active alumni network after graduation. Administrators in the Office of Advancement and Alumni Relations share the same concerns from their respective donor relations and other financial angles.

From the students' perspective, their program closing directly affects their graduation plans, which affects their financial aid, and affects the focus of their studies and research. By redirecting their momentum and motivation, these decisions also potentially derail their mentoring relationships with faculty members who have been advising them throughout their college years. Even if they are able to finish the program before it is terminated, there is a very real chance that faculty members will have to seek employment elsewhere in order to remain gainfully and intellectually employed.

Faculty Members' Concerns

For faculty members, losing a program can interrupt tenure track, promotion, and/or contract renewal plans. Their research and relationships with students, which have progressed and deepened over time, will need to be re-envisioned, and grant funders will need to approve any changes to plans. There are no guarantees that academic work will continue in the same vein, and this truly does feel like a tremendous loss for those invested in the work.

Canceling and teaching out a program might also damage relationships with employers who have provided internships for students and who have subsequently recruited recent graduates into their organizations. The amount of uncertainty for faculty members is distressing, since the decision to close a program has little financial benefit to an institution unless faculty lines are also terminated (Eckel, 2017). This subject has been covered frequently in academic publications, with the primary audience the administrators who must execute such programmatic decisions and manage the subsequent fallout.

Administrators' Concerns

There are some extremely sound reasons for administrators to even consider canceling and then teaching out an academic program.

> When explaining things to the college community, leaders need to work concurrently on the 'what of change' (the decisions), the 'how of change' (the process), and the 'why of change (the case). Of these three, the one that tends to get shortchanged is 'why.' Administrative leaders need to communicate the case for change consistently throughout the process.
>
> (Eckel, 2017, par. 5)

Conversations about program closing tend to occur at many levels within an institution, spanning departments, schools, faculty governance bodies, deans' groups, presidents' cabinet meetings, and academic affairs committee meetings of the governing board. Administrators will likely be called upon – and therefore should be prepared – to answer questions about the institution's identity, vision, and mission:

> What do we value and why do we value it (and what do we no longer value as much)? Who have we been as an institution and who are we going to be? An example of one question asked by leaders of a research university was, 'What does it mean to be a top-tier research university in a state with constrained resources?
> (Eckel, 2017, par. 7)

At the time of this writing, the world is (just barely) emerging from a global pandemic, and the future of institutions of higher education is harder than ever to discern with any degree of confidence. The challenges include revenue losses, tuition and fee refunds, unpredictable enrollment, and reduced state funding, among numerous other competing concerns. The Center for American Progress (Yuen, 2020) provides one example of "the brutal math" that institutions of higher education are confronting due to COVID-19, sharing the following statistics about Rutgers University (a public university system serving more than 71,000 students):

- Rutgers has spent $50 million to repay students for unused campus services such as dining, housing, and parking as a direct result of the pandemic.
- The university system will lose $60 million resulting from canceled surgical procedures at Rutgers medical centers.
- The Rutgers system is losing another $73 million in state appropriations due to a COVID-inspired state spending freeze.

In a related vein, administrators gain leverage when they successfully bring in new donors, large grants, or additional sources of funding. In fact, that is largely how their success is measured by their governing board, so all of the items above will resonate with anyone who's experienced any of these pressures.

The worst case scenario, of course, is for an entire institution to be forced to close its doors due to financial challenges that are simply past the point of no return. In one article in *The Chronicle of Higher Education*, the author noted that he hoped that by sharing his own experience and what he learned throughout the process, that he could help others who may find themselves in a similar, unfortunate position. He shared detailed advice that falls under the following headings:

- Frame the message early and often
- Add humor whenever you can
- Get to know your accreditation and regulatory agencies if you have not already
- Be everyone's chief motivator
- Realize that you are no longer in control of your fate
- Remember that students will watch and learn
- Unplug every now and then

Based on the hierarchical structure of most institutions, the president will be aware of and hold information that they cannot share with all constituent groups. Therefore, it is very important that administrators communicate what they can, when they can, because faculty and staff will be anxious, and students will take their cues from the people they are closest to in the hierarchical structure – faculty members, coaches, tutors, and professional advisors. Consistent communication is therefore critical, as are frequent opportunities for people to share questions and concerns, in person and anonymously (and not just venting in social media outlets). It is important that community members are clear that they are all "in it" together.

Obviously, academic programs are just one category related to institutional resources that administrators and faculty are collectively responsible for, and we've demonstrated how the line that connects programs to resources is not so much a straight line as one that has many off-shoots that connect to other categories, from facilities to personnel to student aid and more. Yet, the question remains: who gets to make the decisions about how resources are allocated?

CULTURAL CURRENCY

Disagreements over the allocation of resources are not new. We experience it in every significant relationship in our lives: with family members, in our workplaces, at community organizations, and among friends. Such disagreements don't always turn acrimonious. Sometimes, they happen because we haven't taken the time to understand each other's perspectives and related expectations about a given situation or decision.

For example, two colleagues traveling to a conference together might have different ideas about how much they're willing to pay for meals and accommodations. One person might be looking forward to some sight-seeing they can squeeze in around the required conference sessions and might have the funds to make that happen. The other person may have a tighter budget, unknown to the other colleague. If they have the foresight and desire to have such a conversation beforehand, they can better understand what each person expects. Otherwise, they may experience several days of frustration if they each think that one person is making decisions that prevent them from the desired sight-seeing or forcing the other to spend more money than that person can comfortably afford. All of this is because they haven't taken the time to understand the perspective of the other, and if an investment in a relationship isn't a priority, then these types of direct conversations may not be necessary. However, if a culture of collegiality is to thrive, then such conversations can open the door to shared experiences, helpful advice, and closer relationships.

Most institutions of higher education have processes in place to make sure that budget and planning are discussed. These processes, meant to be inclusive, do not guarantee full disclosure or authentic participation about the subject of money and personnel, facilities, and operations. Most university budget and planning committees are populated with faculty, staff, and administrators, with occasional committees that include student membership. These committees advise the chief executive officer, typically the president. In theory, every stakeholder group should have input into how an institution's resources are managed. In reality, however, there are some people who have greater influence due to their job/role, which can sometimes leave the rest of the committee members wondering: does my voice even matter?

Foreign Currency Not Recognized

In our survey of faculty and administrators, the most common impasses cited by both cultural groups involved money – specifically, salary, budget priorities, and decisions about spending. Impasses over money were followed closely by impasses related to contracts and the scope of academic work. It is clear that the allocation of resources is a primary source of tension.

Comments from faculty members included:

"In recent years tension has grown between faculty and administration due to resource shortages and efforts by the administration to weaken faculty governance."

"So many of us feel overworked and exhausted. As a result, the work culture is often one of distrust for those who seem to wittingly increase our work loads."

"They keep hiring administrators at hefty salaries and not replacing faculty who have left. Instead they come up with 'temporary' faculty lines and restrict our ability to hire adjunct faculty."

Comments from administrators included:

"Resources, which have always been scarce, continue to decline, and therefore workloads continue to increase. That said, the faculty work tirelessly toward a shared vision."

"I've weathered contentious meetings over budget priorities, openness to change, facing hard questions about resource allocation…it's as predictable as the weather"

"We are a small college, with enrollment of 600. Our work culture is friendly, conscientious, caring. We try to have an open door policy in our offices, and at times, it is difficult to get anything done. I feel I spend an inordinate amount of time just pushing projects forward before I see them come to completion."

As you read and re-read the above comments, what do you notice? For example, it is clear that resources can refer to time as well as money. Are there similarities between the themes that are reflected in the comments, or do they seem to be different? Finding common ground upon which to firmly stand and address topics that increase tension during regular, peaceful times, is one way to practice communicating and listening. In this way, when something unanticipated happens, you have some understanding to build upon, and some currency to trade as needed to reach a compromise in the best interest of students and the institution.

CULTURAL UNIVERSALS

Different cultural groups always have some things that they share or have in common. The term "cultural universals" refers to patterns of behavior or character traits that are visible in all societies around the world. With regard to money and decision-making, decisions about resource allocation were challenging before COVID-19 disrupted various operating procedures around the world. But the pandemic has certainly altered the landscape in significant ways. Discussions between faculty and administrators will be different now than they would have been even just a year ago. The financial precarity of nearly every higher education institution cannot be denied. But each cultural group still brings its own perspective to the negotiating table, and each still needs to make the effort to cultivate an understanding of the other.

Cultural Successes

It is important for your own wellbeing to weave opportunities for gratitude or intention-setting into your work. One skill that can help with many institutional tasks is to practice working toward the primary goal of clearing up misunderstandings. While this may seem simple, when two cultures don't understand each other, then it is much more difficult to work through an impasse. What follows are some examples of sentiments about "success stories," which we provide here to help readers of this book understand their cultural lenses and adjust accordingly. We are intentionally not attributing these quotes to the cultural group represented by the person who made these comments. In this way, we invite you to notice your hunches and your biases or assumptions.

"Faculty believed the institution was spending extra money on campus beautification to impress the trustees. This was cleared up when it was explained that it was a part of the maintenance contract with a vendor."

"Two faculty did not have enough students signed up for a London program in order to make it self-supporting. Administrators helped them extend the sign-up period and advertise the opportunity, then filled in the much smaller amount needed after four more students signed up."

"Pay did not increase in kind, but we lowered the number of students required to 'make' a class."

As mentioned previously, the overarching goal that we – the authors – have is to provide examples that help you cultivate the capacity to understand the perspective of others in your higher education setting. We know that faculty and administrators share an overarching goal – to provide high-quality education to students who therefore contribute to a compassionate and productive society. We may sometimes disagree about how to utilize and allocate resources, but we can always anchor the work in teaching and learning.

The discussion questions below provide starting points for you to explore your own assumptions and imagine actionable steps to move beyond those assumptions. We also encourage you to discuss these questions with members of your own educational group culture and across groups, to gain familiarity with each other and build "muscle" and confidence to consider new/unfamiliar perspectives. This is how you start to build trust.

SUMMARY

Resources in higher education can include the most obvious – money – as well as time, personnel, and facilities. Faculty members and administrators tend to disagree about how resources are to be allocated, and these tensions are exacerbated during times of crisis. Due to the roles and information that faculty and administrators have, it is helpful when communication informs an appreciation for a different perspective. Recognizing these perspectives and applying the understanding that comes from intercultural communication can transform the academic environment into a healthier one for all community members.

PRACTICE AND REFLECTION

1. Consider a current (or past) disagreement about the allocation of resources at your university. What power are you assuming the other party has in this situation? Who can be your guide to help you understand if your assumption about power is accurate?
2. What are some resources in your institution that could be labeled "material resources," and what are some resources that could be labeled "non-material resources"? Describe any differences in how these types of resources are valued in your workplace. How can you tell that some are valued more than others? Do you agree with the values assigned to these resources? If not, what would you change?
3. In his article, Hoyle (2009) advised presidents to "add humor" as often as possible to diffuse tensions in the face of an unpleasant inevitability. Can you remember a time when humor broke down barriers in a faculty–administrator impasse, or simply during a tense meeting? What are some other strategies that seem to work well in your setting to lift the spirits of the institutional citizens?

RESOURCES

Library of Congress Digital Collections

https://www.loc.gov/collections/?fa=subject:oral+histories

The Library of Congress website can distract you from workplace tensions for weeks. This particular section of the website provides visitors with myriad resources that are inspiring and informational. You can explore cultural perspectives on a host of topics and also gain understanding about the influence of time on perennial challenges in society.

A Joke a Day

https://www.ajokeaday.com/

Looking to infuse some humor in a meeting to lower the levels of frustration and lift people's moods? This website features a daily joke, as well as archives of thousands of jokes assorted thematically. All jokes on this site are "clean" and family-friendly.

Throwing in the Towel

https://www.psychologytoday.com/us/blog/how-be-yourself/201907/7-reasons-feel-confident-about-throwing-in-the-towel

This article provides additional links to more resources and presents the concept of the "sunk cost fallacy" (familiar in situations related to psychology and economics) – a decision-making bias that contributes to people investing numerous kinds of resources into an effort because they are already engaged in the work/project. Strategies to disentangle oneself and to reframe the notions of "persistence" and "giving up" are provided.

REFERENCES

Eckel, P.D. (2017, November 17). What to consider when closing an academic program. *The Chronicle of Higher Education, 64*(12), 19.

Goodman, P. (2021, April 18). The 8 main reasons for war. *Owlcation*. Retrieved at https://owlcation.com/social-sciences/The-Main-Reasons-For-War

Hoyle, M.J. (2009, January). How does a president shut down a college? *The Chronicle of Higher Education, 55*(19), A60.

Pérez-Villanueva, S. (2021). #MeToo in early modern Spain: Visual pleasures and silence breakers. In B.L. Gasior & M.E. Badía (Eds.), *Reconsidering early modern Spanish literature* (pp. 106–128). Juan de la Cuesta – Hispanic Monographs.

Spiliakos, A. (2019, February 6). Tragedy of the commons: What it is and 5 examples. *Harvard School of Business Online*. Retrieved at https://online.hbs.edu/blog/post/tragedy-of-the-commons-impact-on-sustainability-issues

Whitford, E. (2020, March 30). Bay area university works to stave off a closure. *Inside Higher Ed*. Retrieved at https://www.insidehighered.com/news/2020/03/30/%E2%80%98it-would-take-something-major%E2%80%99-keep-doors-open-notre-dame-de-namur

Yuen, V. (2020, June 11). Mounting peril for public higher education during the coronavirus pandemic. *Center for American Progress*. Retrieved at https://www.americanprogress.org/issues/education-postsecondary/reports/2020/06/11/485963/mounting-peril-public-higher-education-coronavirus-pandemic/

Zheng, L. (2019, June 17). *Students, alumni fight closure of OU's organ technology, repair program*. Retrieved at https://kfor.com/news/students-alumni-fight-closure-of-ous-organ-technology-repair/

Chapter Six

Cultural Priority: Territory

The topic of territory is one that is often associated with disputes –most often with war – and the conditions leading up to and sustaining territorial conflicts are analyzed from every angle (Dzurek, 2005; Goodman, 2021). The subject has always held tremendous appeal in the news media, as evident in the frequency of reports that consume air-time and print space during territorial disputes that have global interest and impact. Throughout history, territorial conflicts have escalated into war, and simultaneous concerns continue to exist about how information about such conflicts is being shared with the public while conflicts are ongoing and evolving (Elders, 2005).

The metaphor of territory is sometimes tossed about during difficult conversations among administrators and faculty members, particularly with reference to academic purview, which we will discuss later in the chapter. But the learning that has been acquired by scholars who analyze territorial disputes is not often applied in institutions of higher education. Ironically, the field of education is presumed to be distinct from political and military domains, when the lived experience in higher education is so often described using wartime terminology (Walker, 2014).

THE TAXONOMY OF TERRITORY

Research investigating territory centers around some simple, yet complex questions about territory: "What makes territory important? More significantly, what makes some territory more important than other territory?" (Dzurek, 2005, p. 263). If administrators and faculty can better understand the "tangible and symbolic dimensions of territorial disputes," (p. 263) they will gain greater clarity about how to best address territory in their academic settings. Some characteristics related to territory, and what happens when territory is perceived to be under threat, will be readily familiar, such as negotiations and compromise, "armed" conflict (e.g., protests/petitions, threats

CULTURAL PRIORITY: TERRITORY

related to resources), and overlapping or unclear boundaries that contribute to tensions. As you read the following case study, see if you can identify territory and values associated with the territory on different sides of the dispute. What steps could have prevented the surprise experience by administrators and the resentment felt by faculty members?

> **CASE STUDY: VENTURING INTO THE REALM OF ONLINE INSTRUCTION**
>
> Asiya pulled up the email invitation that had gone out from the university provost, "cordially inviting all faculty members to a town hall meeting with members of the Office of Academic Affairs to discuss plans for online learning and instruction." According to the invitation, the provost "welcomes input from the faculty about their experiences with online instruction."
>
> "If they really wanted our input, they wouldn't wait until Friday afternoon at 5 pm to send these emails!" Asiya said to herself, taking a sip of coffee. "One day, I'm bringing wine in a white paper coffee cup," she thought. "No one would know! Or maybe Mike can make some of those 'special' brownies he's always mentioning. Anything to get through these meetings!" She smiled to herself, knowing that this would be yet another one of so many frustrating meetings like she'd sat through before.
>
> She saw Mike enter the room and look around until he saw her. She waved to him and pointed to the seat next to her, which she'd saved for him. He rolled his eyes and hustled over to her, squeezing past the clusters of faculty talking animatedly with each other.
>
> "Sooooo...the Office of Academic Affairs can decide what the university's post-pandemic online strategy should be? What's even the point?" Mike asked, with his familiar quizzical/furrowed brow expression that always reminded Asiya of her youngest brother's facial expressions.
>
> "Wait –" Mike said, putting his hand on Asiya's shoulder as he looked at his cellphone. "Alana just texted and said that the provost invited some third-party vendor to give a presentation at this meeting."
>
> "Oh, for f***'s sake, this decision is already a done deal." Asiya groaned.
>
> The provost walked to the front of the room and signaled to a group of unfamiliar young people standing together along the wall decorated with the portraits of past board chairs. The people picked up baskets adorned with colorful bows and circulated throughout

the room, handing small bags filled with chocolate goodies and a vendor-branded stress ball to the faculty members.

"Is this an omen?" Mike asked and then cackled raspily.

"What's next? Wine and cheese?" Asiya added, leaning toward him and gently elbowing him in the ribs.

The provost projected his presentation onto the screen against the wall and silenced the group by reminding them of the $4 million budget deficit from the previous fiscal year – presented in colorful, graphic detail – and the new challenges brought about because of the pandemic. He thanked everyone for their hard work and flexibility during such an *unprecedented* time.

"To help us navigate the 'new normal,' I sought the advice of a highly respected VP of enrollment management from [my previous institution]. Together, we invited experts from a leading provider of best-in-class technology-enabled solutions to help us see what's possible here." The provost smiled proudly and gestured toward the group of young people, who were once again gathered along the portrait wall.

The smiling and nodding group of young people reminded Asiya of a team of Olympic athletes – they all looked young, healthy, and beautiful. A man stood up from his seat against the portrait wall and thanked the provost for such a kind introduction. The two men shook hands, and the provost handed the PowerPoint remote to the VP. Asiya couldn't keep up with the details of the polished presentation.

"So many slick infographics that are supposed to inspire confidence and awe!" she thought to herself. The VP mentioned that he had previously worked for a for-profit online education company, and that's when Asiya stopped listening. Occasional words and phrases permeated her consciousness: "wide range of enterprise solutions…customized for diverse business needs…data-driven products…innovative strategies…thank you for listening."

She perked up when Mike poked her leg with his stylus. The VP and the reps were leaving the room and the provost thanked them again "for taking the time to share such insightful marketplace realities with the group." He watched them leave with a smile plastered on his face.

The provost turned back to the faculty audience and grasped the edges of the podium. He leaned toward the microphone and said quietly,

> We've been presented with an opportunity that we're really excited to share with you. In the president's cabinet meeting this morning, we were talking about how we've experienced such

CULTURAL PRIORITY: TERRITORY

success with the recent conversion to online classes during the pandemic. You all made amazing strides during an *unprecedented* time. Just because we'll be resuming more face-to-face classes this fall, that doesn't mean that we need to abandon what we started. We're looking to partner with a third-party vendor to scale up the development of our online programs.

He paused, slowly looking across the room, from one side of the room to the other.

Asiya looked around the room as well, to get a sense for the general sentiment. She noticed her dean, smiling twitchily, and the sycophantic business professor nodding approvingly. "Must he always wear that Wharton sweatshirt?" she thought to herself. "We're all teaching *here* now."

After a few tense moments of silence, the provost called on one faculty member, and then it snowballed into a cascade of questions, one after the other – loudly, pell-mell – with people not waiting for the provost to respond before calling out their questions:

- "I literally just read an article that said this exact vendor is being investigated for something shady. Have we looked into this? We haven't signed a contract, have we?"
- "What's the revenue split? Why would we give them so much when they're not actually creating anything?"
- "Who *owns* this curriculum? What about intellectual property?"
- "How does this get negotiated with the collective bargaining agreement? How does this affect our workload?"

There were many questions blurted out and very few answers provided. The provost's assistant was feverishly taking notes on her laptop – sitting up very straight on the edge of her chair.

After the meeting, the provost and the VP of enrollment management reunited in the hall and exchanged pleasantries before heading out with the group of young people, who seemed to move in a pack.

"I bet they're headed into town for a steak dinner and drinks – all of which they can pay for and write off as a business expense!" Mike chortled. They heard the provost say to the VP, "I think it went really well!" The twitchy dean scampered past them quickly, walking fast to catch up with the provost.

"How about some margaritas and nachos?" Asiya asked Josh. She held up her goodie bag and said, laughing, "We already have dessert!"

In Dzurek's (2005) research, referenced at the beginning of this chapter, he identifies six items that he includes in a matrix to evaluate the "intensifying factors" he considers useful in evaluating territorial disputes. These include "cultural differences," "weak government," and "third-party involvement." These items parallel administrator and faculty tensions in higher education, related to culture, governance (discussed in Chapter Seven), and vendors or consultant groups that are brought into the culture to provide input into a matter identified as important by the upper administrators and/or governing board. As you read and process the following perspectives expressed by faculty and administrators, see if you see (or "hear") evidence of these items in the responses. How might awareness of the others' perspectives help these academic community members to discuss important matters without so much anger and defensiveness? How can these conversations occur in ways that don't feel like territorial violations?

ADMINISTRATOR S'S PERSPECTIVE

What follows is the reaction of a composite administrator, created by integrating reactions from focus group participants, survey respondents, and conversations with professional colleagues in higher education settings.

"Online programs can be a great source of necessary revenue. Every institution has to have a few cash cows – programs that can be delivered at low cost and that bring in the money. Those cash cows help support the boutique programs that are part of our mission as an educational institution."

"Going online gets complicated when it gets mixed in with an outside, for-profit vendor. I'm not necessarily a fan of using an outside vendor. In fact, when I was dean at a university that entered into a partnership like that, I held firm and said my particular school wouldn't be part of that. I paid dearly for that among the administration, but earned the respect of faculty. We created our own hybrid program in-house – one that blended some online courses with short-term face-to-face programming designed by the faculty."

"Some administrators push to outsource with for-profit companies because those vendors will take on the arduous, costly tasks of marketing, recruiting, and some advising. They also take a slice of the revenue, of course. To be honest, sometimes administrators are forced into these deals. Faculty assume that provosts or presidents can make certain changes or wield certain power, but often they can't. There are times when there are deals or partnerships put in place in the past, and

I would rather make some changes, but I know that if I do then a donor might pull funding that is critical to our operation. If that happened, then we'd have to make cuts – and faculty would get mad that we're cutting programs."

"These kinds of partnerships and programs stir up territory disputes because faculty want to (and should!) govern anything related to academics, but those border lines get blurry. At one of my previous universities, one woman was making decisions about how to assess and give credit to potential students based on Prior Learning Assessments – giving students credit for their work experience. This one woman was deciding who gets credit for what, with no clarity about her process and with no one else involved. She didn't even have people's CVs on hand to inform or defend her decisions about credit. She considered it her territory, but I had to take over and do some major cleanup – and I'm sure I was viewed as the one encroaching on someone else's territory."

FACULTY MEMBER K'S PERSPECTIVE

What follows is the reaction of a composite faculty member, created by integrating reactions from focus group participants, survey respondents, and conversations with professional colleagues in higher education settings.

"Many years ago, our dean was getting pressure to put some of the curriculum online. We started with *one* program, developing online versions of all of the courses in that program. Then, we did the same thing for one course in *every* program. As faculty, we resisted and pushed back. To put a course online we were asked to shorten the timeframe of the course from the usual 16 weeks to eight weeks, because we were told that's what the market research tells us students want. But you can't possibly have the same learning experience in half the time. Meanwhile, I heard an administrator bragging about bringing in more money because of the program."

"I agree that online classes can help expand access and affordability. But some of the for-profit programs clearly don't prioritize quality. People who aren't scholars and who don't understand pedagogy are the ones making decisions and often designing syllabi. And it's hard to get a good outside partner."

"We were in a relationship for years with a sub-standard entity. Faculty and most deans thought entering this relationship was a terrible idea, but the president wanted it. It never worked well, we lost millions, yet we were locked into that relationship for years. The company had promised great marketing and said they would provide success coaching. They were admitting students of lower caliber, and then they provided crappy supports. We kept wondering, 'why can't we do it ourselves? Why do we need an outside entity?' Some people even joked that the president must've had a 'love child' who worked for that for-profit."

"You have to do online really well in order to stand out, but that's not our core mission. If our university is known for a particular boutique program, but we push that aside in favor of these other programs that have nothing to do with our brand or the people we have on faculty, then we're killing our own institution. I was in a meeting with people from one of the third-party vendors. They had a menu of programs that they identified through market research, including museum studies and business – not our territory. It didn't make any sense. So, our administrators were not just pushing us to take our existing classes online, but they were pushing us to go online with programs we'd never even had before. It made no sense."

"That said, with COVID-19 forcing the issue, I have seen some of the benefits of being online. We have a faculty member who teaches dance and movement classes. These sound like the type of classes you would need to conduct in person. But he's been able to use video with students in their own settings so they could record and share with the group things that they never would have been able to do in a class setting. He's excited about what the technology was able to help him do with his class. Personally, when I see the little postage-stamp sized faces on my Zoom screen, some tension melts away because that's why I'm here. I do believe that administrators see it that way too, at the core. That's what we do."

How can expectations around boundaries, values, and decision-making be clarified in higher education contexts? In the following sections, we explore cultural elements that can inform your own consideration of territory and academic purview.

TERRITORY IN CONTEXT

Tensions about territory in higher education contexts typically center around academic purview – who has authority over course content and delivery, program offerings, and grading, among other elements included under the broad umbrella of teaching and learning. While the varieties of administrator and faculty tensions within an institution are well known and studied, Levin (2006) suggests that "confining cultural conflict to internal antagonisms is too narrow" (p. 64). He notes that "the government or those representing special interest groups, including business and industry" can have influence on institutional culture that at times prevents administrators and faculty from being an "integrated unit" (p. 64).

While funding and legislative rules and restrictions are elements that can be considered somewhat "tangible," though confusing at times, there are less tangible aspects of territory that contribute to tensions between administrators and faculty. Journalists have written about the "human condition" of territoriality, such as a piece in the *Los Angeles Times* that describes how humans are motivated by the need for "space, security, or status" (Tomashoff, 1992, par. 9). This is interesting for everyday readers because people enact these territorial behaviors every day (e.g., "saving" a seat so that you can have extra room, sitting in the same seat in a classroom every class). Researchers in the social sciences have been writing about territoriality for decades, as a "fundamental human activity" distinguishable by:

- types of territory – public territories, home territories, interactional territories, and body territories
- territorial encroachment – violation, invasion, and contamination
- reaction to encroachment – turf defense, insulation, and linguistic collusion (Lyman & Scott, 1967)

It is fascinating that in spite of society's cross-disciplinary knowledge about these challenges – knowledge that informs us about the human condition – we continue to fall into patterns of behavior that contribute to unpleasant territorial workplace struggles. And as much as administrators and faculty attempt to reduce tensions by keeping students' needs at the core of their work, students are not immune to the impact of territorial disputes between administrators and faculty members and have their own influence on and perspective related to territory.

Students' Concerns

One very concrete example, such as when federal or state aid is reduced, results in a situation where students lose critical funding that could support their educational pursuits. Students and their families typically find their financial aid packages to be very confusing, and there are so many terms and overlapping entities that factor into specific arrangements for individual students that they often feel completely overwhelmed. This is similar to what many people experience related to health care and insurance – terms are so confusing that people feel helpless to help themselves and may not be able to best advocate for themselves and choose a viable course of action.

Although they would likely not recognize it as such, this type of experience illustrates the term "linguistic collusion," in that a negative association with the language/discourse leads some to believe – rightly or mistakenly – that terms or jargon are purposely used to prevent people from accessing their resources or keeping people in a state of disenfranchisement. Whether or not they would characterize the experience as linguistic collusion, students absolutely struggle to cover financial costs quite often, and therefore, they sometimes choose a less expensive course modality, typically a shorter-term, online offering, to meet program requirements. This practice opens the door for subsequent frustrations that faculty members express, when courses from for-profit companies are accepted as transfer credits for university programs, and faculty do not feel that the for-profit course content reflects the same quality and rigor as the comparable courses offered in their own on-campus programs.

Faculty Members' Concerns

For many faculty members, what feels "at stake" related to the debate about online learning rests squarely at the center of academics and pedagogy. Faculty believe in a shared mission to provide students with a high-quality education that, in turn, contributes to a more compassionate and productive society. Then, faculty contend, it follows that what defines a quality education is a decision that resides with the faculty.

Faculty are familiar with accreditation processes as one way to identify and measure quality with objective standards, but they also have related concerns about the quality of accreditation and questions about who can be trusted to ensure that valuable standards are met.

It's hard for faculty to trust others when it comes to academic integrity, particularly outside partners, but decisions about entering into partnerships typically rest with administrators.

Administrators' Concerns

Administrators contend that an institution's shared mission also emphasizes the *reach* of a high-quality education if it is expected to contribute to society in meaningful, equitable ways. Who decides how access is achieved? One of the benefits of online programs is that they significantly expand access to education and to potential revenue streams that will support non-revenue-generating aspects of the university.

Administrators argue simply that this is why the decision rests within their territory. But one of the fallbacks is that student retention is harder when students don't have direct access to the on-campus experience, which includes support services such as tutoring, career advising, mental health and wellness programming, as well as social activities. During the initial

COVID-19 lockdown and subsequent scramble to convert face-to-face experiences into online experiences, many administrators accelerated their prior plans about their institution's growth into digital learning territory and/or relationships with the for-profit sector.

THE BOUNDARY BETWEEN BUSINESS AND ACADEMIA

New reports are making their way into the mainstream, describing what one author calls "The alarming rise in for-profit college enrollment" (Cellini, 2020). There is a difference between: (a) an institution creating its own menu of offerings that provide access to degree programs in different modalities, and (b) a fully online company that profits from its development and rollout of course offerings that appeal to a mass market, whether or not these programs lead to a degree or are courses that may be taken "a la carte." Once again, the tension between educational and economic values is evident.

Some noteworthy statistics include:

- For first-time students, enrollment in for-profit institutions rose by 13% among first-time students aged 21–24 and rose by 15% among those aged 25–29. In contrast, enrollment for the same age groups in four-year public institutions declined over 20%.
- Among full-time students enrolled in for-profit college programs, 74% of first-time, full-time students take out student loans. This is significantly higher than the 21% at community colleges and 47% in four-year public institutions who borrow money to cover costs.
- Students who take out student loans to pay for for-profit program costs also accumulate more debt than their peers – approximately $8,000/year. Students taking out loans average approximately $4,700 in loans for community college costs and approximately $7,000 to support the costs of programs at four-year public institutions of higher education (Cellini, 2020).

Statistics like these have prompted investigations and subsequent lawsuits (e.g., The Project on Predatory Student Lending at Harvard Law School). In spite of criticism, some third-party for-profit vendors hold appeal for administrators because they defray costs associated with marketing academic programs, theoretically spending millions of dollars that the institutions otherwise couldn't afford. However, these arrangements often include financial incentives that result in the vendor receiving a large portion of any enrollment revenue linked directly to their marketing outreach.

This often results in admissions staff being pressured to accept students that they typically would not accept, due to lack of academic preparedness and/or demonstrated ability across several measures. Once students are accepted into the institution's "system," then they become "our students," which some faculty wryly translate into "our problem."

In times when financial resources are plentiful, morale tends to be high and faculty and administrators enjoy more frequent opportunities to experiment or take risks with curriculum or program development. In times of financial crisis or trimming, faculty tend to feel that they can't do anything without navigating through multiple layers of permission. It's tough, and some compromises feel less than ideal. Faculty feel attached to – and invested in – curriculum because they are the academic experts and design what they think is best for students. Administrators sometimes complain about faculty being "purists" and also don't like to conceive of students as simply "consumers."

A faculty member in our study shared an example in which an associate dean required faculty to cut what was considered to be an introductory course from the program of study for a Master's degree program. The administrator argued that the credit total was too high, and they couldn't compete in the market with such a high credit total for the program. He reasoned that they could instead make the introductory course a prerequisite for the program. Therefore, accepted students who had taken a similar course in their undergraduate studies would be able to waive the requirement, and those who didn't have the prior coursework would be able to take that class during the summer before they began the program. Faculty argued that this simply increased the financial burden for some students and didn't ultimately reduce the credit total at all. While the compromise was made, the faculty did not feel comfortable about the decision and felt that the associate dean had forced their hands, violating the academic integrity of the program and academic purview of the faculty. The associate dean also didn't feel so good about that decision, but felt that it was made in order to save the program as a whole. The ultimate test of any decision, such as the one described above, is evident in donor funding that an administrator is able to garner from philanthropists and/or foundations whose officers believe in an institution's programs and mission, as well as the student enrollment that occurs as a result.

THE BOUNDARY BETWEEN ACADEMICS AND THE COLLEGE EXPERIENCE

Throughout the recent pandemic, much conversation and debate ensued about whether or not college can be the same without an on-campus experience. This conversation is not new, of course, as the debate about course delivery models has been around since the days when correspondence courses were taken using "snail mail" or over the radio (Kentnor, 2015). The values inherent in discussion and debate relate to how knowledge is delivered and received, as well as the return on investment. It also raises questions about what people really expect for (and from) their money.

The American system of college education is rooted in the English tradition of Oxford and Cambridge, valuing the residential experience just as much as – or even as inseparable from – the academic experience. Consider this, from Ian Bogost in *The Atlantic*:

> When Western universities got their start in medieval Europe, they were integrated into major cities, such as Paris, Prague, and Milan. England was an exception. Its oldest colleges, Oxford and Cambridge, were nestled into the bucolic countryside. When Harvard became the first college in the future United States, it adopted the English notion of a campus as a place apart.
>
> (Bogost, 2020, par. 10)

Bogost notes that even in big cities, colleges

> see and sell themselves as hamlets decoupled from the rest of the world. They need to maintain that myth in order to provide the college experience in undiluted form—even while they also host massive flows of people, ideas, and capital in and out of their gates.
>
> (par. 12)

For administrators attempting to manage their campuses during the ever-changing COVID-19 crisis, bringing students back to campus in a safe way was a priority for reasons related to finances and safety. In terms of finances, operating budgets depend on auxiliary on-campus fees such as dining plan costs and dorm fees. Fixed costs are, by their very nature, the same regardless of whether anyone is living on campus. If institutions have dorms, that means that they also have providers for debt servicing, contracts with food vendors, and facilities maintenance costs tied to electricity, heat, water, and more. Those costs exist, period.

Some critics (e.g., campus employees, students' family members) accused administrators of being "money-grubbing" and putting people at risk by prioritizing students returning to campus. But many administrators argued that because they had such a strong COVID mitigation plan in place, their campuses were actually a safer space for people to be. Throughout the COVID-19 evolution, there was a trend for greater transmission off campus and in the surrounding communities. As a result of statistics trending in positive directions for campuses across much of the United States, a track record of trust now exists that will provide a reference point for academic communities in the future.

BUILDING TRUST HAS ITS BENEFITS

One provost in our research study described a conversation he recently had with a faculty senate president. The faculty senate president shared that a number of faculty in a particular department were feeling harshly judged by an email that had been sent by one of the deans, who had cited a lack of compliance with a seemingly obscure policy. The dean had apparently invoked the name of the provost as the one who was demanding compliance. Some faculty were agitating to start a petition. Fortunately, this particular faculty senate president had a sufficient level of trust with the provost to bring up the issue.

The provost shared with us that he immediately flashed back to a meeting he had recently had with the deans and realized that either the dean had completely misunderstood the directive, or the faculty member had misunderstood the dean. The provost realized that this could be further complicated by a long-standing personality conflict that had been inadvertently reignited. A decade ago, this provost had been a faculty member in that same department and so had intimate knowledge of the characters. He knew well how the entire situation could quickly escalate beyond the simple misunderstanding. He told us that he first returned to his office to guzzle a bit of Pepto-Bismol and then proceeded with a plan to intervene. Before the day was done, the provost had wandered over to chat with the errant dean, casually mentioning what he had learned (without sharing the source) and providing some tips for how the dean might correct the misperception. He then followed up by having a chat with a well-respected program chair and casually brought up the situation. He asked the chair to try and assuage the concerns of the faculty by providing the larger context.

Without the trusting relationship between the faculty senate president and provost, there would have been no intervention. Furthermore, without the relational conversation skills of the provost, and a willing faculty program chair, this also could have escalated into a full-blown episode. This example illustrates the vital importance of trust, emotional intelligence, and capacity of administrators and faculty to engage in dialogue when there is a misunderstanding. Sadly, it is often the case that there is limited trust and limited capacity for conversations that lead to mutual understanding. These types of relationship-building conversations do not occur as frequently as would be most helpful to an institution. Sometimes this is due to the busy schedules that make it difficult to arrange mutually convenient conversations, sometimes this is due to the frequency with which administrators change jobs in higher education, and sometimes it is simply due to clashing cultures.

Conversations and "face time" in numerous meetings doesn't guarantee a positive result: people are people, after all. But if administrators and faculty members do not actively seek ways to connect with and understand each other, then cultural misunderstandings in higher education are more likely to grow into large-scale territorial battles. Dzurek (2005) "attempted to capture the complexity and subtlety of territorial disputes and the factors that might influence how they are perceived" and noted that the "strength of the approach lies in the transparency of the process" (Dzurek, 2005, p. 273). Trust does not exist by accident. It's built with small wins and relationships over time. In the chapter that follows, we examine governance in higher education and explore some of the ways intercultural perspectives can contribute to healthier communities.

SUMMARY

Territory is a cultural priority for administrators and faculty members and has been studied as part of the human condition for decades. While there are distinct types of territory, and reactions when territory is perceived to be violated, there are also ways to recognize shared interests and build trust. Recognizing different perspectives during territorial disputes is critical in order to establish practices that resonate within an institutional community as respectful and responsive, affirming people's connection to place.

PRACTICE AND REFLECTION

1. Take some time to reflect on what claims to territory you experience in your setting. What are some of the values that you can articulate, which motivate you to advocate for your position in a given situation? Consider tangible as well as intangible types of territory as you reflect (e.g., budget, ideas).
2. Imagine you have been told (by someone in a position of power above your level of authority) that you must convert 75% of all academic offerings to an online modality. What are some arguments that you can make in favor of such a requirement, such as increased access or affordability, and what are some arguments against this idea (e.g., quality of experience)? Think about how you would

prioritize the ideas that come to mind, and how you might frame a conversation with someone to learn more about this decision-making process and some potential consequences that could occur as a result of the change.
3. Imagine how different teaching and learning would be if academic programs relied on postal delivery or radio broadcasts. What gains have been made as a result of stepping into new territory afforded by educational technology? What compromises have been made? How are institutions more vulnerable as a result?

RESOURCES

Geography – Territoriality

https://geography.name/territoriality/

This website presents information about territoriality from several vantage points, including geography and psycho-social factors that include the inherent tension that exists between humans' natural inclination toward movement and the contradictory need to feel fixed in the sense of place and connection to others.

Psychology Research & Reference: Territoriality

http://psychology.iresearchnet.com/social-psychology/group/territoriality/

Presenting clear and insightful definitions of different types of territoriality, as well as behaviors related to territoriality (e.g., infringements, defenses), this website makes some concepts quite tangible. In this way, it is easy to see the direct connections between perceptions of a violation of one's territory and the reactions people may have due to their understanding of physical space, ideas, and other kinds of territory. Some small, helpful shifts in behavior and communication can make workplace conflicts much less challenging.

Mister Rogers' Neighborhood (Episodes 1712 and 1713) – "Sharing"

https://www.imdb.com/title/tt2664372/?ref_=tt_ep_pr
https://www.imdb.com/title/tt2664354/?ref_=tt_ep_nx

These episodes, which aired in February 1997 on PBS, feature different types of sharing – sharing resources and sharing ideas. Interpersonal conflicts are presented and discussed in the friendly, judgment-free manner emblematic of Mr. Rogers and the other program regulars. While the television program is designed for young children, the lessons learned are valuable to humans of all ages. These episodes are typically available for viewing through public library online services, "on-demand" PBS cable stations, YouTube, and the Mister Rogers' Neighborhood website (https://misterrogers.org/watch/).

REFERENCES

Bogost, I. (2020, October 20). America will sacrifice anything for the college experience, *The Atlantic*. Retrieved at https://www.theatlantic.com/technology/archive/2020/10/college-was-never-about-education/616777/

Cellini, S.R. (2020, November 2). The alarming rise in for-profit college enrollment. *Brookings*. Retrieved at https://www.brookings.edu/blog/brown-center-chalkboard/2020/11/02/the-alarming-rise-in-for-profit-college-enrollment/

Dzurek, D.J. (2005). What makes territory important: Tangible and intangible dimensions. *GeoJournal, 64*, 263–274.

Elders, C. (2005). Media under fire: Fact and fiction in conditions of war. *International Review of the Red Cross, 87*(860), 639–648.

Goodman, P. (2021, April 18). The 8 main reasons for war. *Owlcation*. Retrieved at https://owlcation.com/social-sciences/The-Main-Reasons-For-War

Kentnor, H. (2015). Distance education and the evolution of online learning in the United States. *Curriculum and Teaching Dialogue, 17*(1 & 2), 21–34.

Levin, J.S. (2006, January/February). Faculty work: Tensions between educational and economic values. *The Journal of Higher Education, 77*(1), 62–88.

Lyman, S.M., & Scott, M.B. (1967, Autumn). Territoriality: A neglected sociological dimension. *Social Problems, 15*(2), 236–249.

The Project on Predatory Student Lending. (n.d.). *Legal Services Center of Harvard Law School (LSC)*. Retrieved at https://predatorystudentlending.org/about-the-project/

Tomashoff, C. (1992, September 22). The human condition/why we're territorial: Get outta my space. *The Los Angeles Times*. Retrieved at https://www.latimes.com/archives/la-xpm-1992-09-22-vw-1113-story.html

Walker, J. (2014, July 23). Trench talk: A guide to first world war slang. *The Guardian*. https://www.theguardian.com/education/2014/jul/23/first-world-war-slang-glossary

Chapter Seven

Cultural Priority: Governance

Over 800 years have passed since the chancellor of the University of Paris issued a legal document "confirmed by the Pope...that he was obliged to obtain the vote of professors in matters connected with the appointments for the teaching of theology" (Shattock, 2006, p. 1), yet governance in institutions of higher education "remains a contested subject and one which is still evolving to fit a changing environment" (p. 1). As education has become more international in scope and reach, the topic of governance has been studied in a global context that invites comparison and opportunities for transformation (e.g., Dobbins, Knill, & Vögtle, 2011; Paradeise, Reale, & Goastellec, 2009).

TIME AND TIDE WAIT FOR NO INSTITUTION

Like all organizations, institutions of higher education do not function without rules and systems management, and they are also held to quality standards and mandates. Governance is assumed to be working well when various levels of governance function together effectively (Shattock, 2006). The different levels of governance in a university setting most often flow "right through the institution from a governing body, down through senates and academic boards to faculty boards and departmental meetings" (p. 1).

While the hierarchical structure of university governance lends itself to clarity in terms of design and direction, the theoretical approaches to understanding what could be perceived as a simple design are much more opaque. Some researchers focus on the "administrative, economical, and juridical aspects" of governance, including:

- how a public or private institution is "internally structured and governed"
- how the institution "is legally embedded in its working environment and/or its operational systems" and
- "how it cooperates with external parties" (p. 2)

CULTURAL PRIORITY: GOVERNANCE

Another framework for examining institutional governance focuses the lens more closely on educational factors such as "higher education expenditures, higher education enrollment, higher education expenditures per student, literacy rate, research and development expenditures and economic growth" (Zaman, 2015, p. 1).

Some of the difficulty in exploring governance in a straightforward manner resides in the tension that exists because higher education in Western countries and societies is embedded in specific historical and socio-political contexts, and therefore, related practices stem from traditions and mindsets, accordingly (e.g., many European countries, North and South America, and regions that were under British rule at some point in time). The very concept of "Western" culture or society grew out of a very specific historical and religious tradition, replete with biases and assumptions that have continued to exist in these practices and traditions. Some current research has opened channels for discourse and critique, challenging systems of oppression and colonization that have perpetuated ways of thinking, ways of being, that have resulted in centuries of oppression. Arguing that institutions of higher education are "large systems of authoritative control," Mbembe (2016) impels readers to:

> decolonize the systems of access and management insofar as they have turned higher education into a marketable product, rated, bought and sold by standard units, measured, counted and reduced to staple equivalence by impersonal, mechanical tests and therefore readily subject to statistical consistency, with numerical standards and units. We have to decolonize this because it is deterring students and teachers from a free pursuit of knowledge.
> (p. 30)

As mentioned throughout this book, the challenges facing higher education, and the tensions that exist between faculty and administrators, have evolved over time and yet the very existence of challenges and tensions has remained consistent. Mbembe eloquently questions whether the call for decolonization is, in fact, potentially futile because we are "fighting a complexly mutating entity with concepts inherited from an entirely different age and epoch" (p. 32). How can faculty and administrators pause to focus and address challenges in the moment, when those very challenges are constantly changing due to internal and external factors such as the ones noted above? Faculty and administrators must wrestle with the cultural priorities of resources, territory, governance, and tradition as they always have. When governance tensions rise to the surface, the other priorities remain simultaneously and intricately woven into the fabric of the institution. Depending on the issue of the moment, that fabric can feel comforting, warm, or just plain itchy.

CASE STUDY: GOVERNING THROUGH UNCERTAINTY

Miriam scrolled through the hundreds of emails she archived, which she'd barely had time to glance at during March 2020. These included emails from subscription sites like *The New York Times* and BBC News, among others. Those particular email subject lines made her shudder involuntarily: Wuhan, China shut down; Iran and Italy reeling; Spain on lockdown; Germany's and Canada's borders closed – all of Europe "closed." Notifications hitting closer to home announced the NBA suspending its season and Broadway going dark. And then, of course, the email that she'd had to send out to the university community in early March, telling students not to return after spring break, and that coursework would continue remotely until further notice.

It hardly seemed possible that a year had passed, since every day felt at the same time to last for a minute and a month. Her world had been consumed with information – every university, every administrator, every faculty member, every staff member, and every student and family was experiencing chaos: logistical, emotional, financial, professional, and, of course, health-related chaos. It was so hard to balance all of the competing information and evolving expert guidance.

A lot of decision-making had happened on the fly during this period, understandably. Hard decisions had to be made fast. Inevitably, there had been a lot of movement within the top ranks at several institutions, with several high-level resignations in quick succession, followed by new executives being brought on board in rapid fashion. Next came announcements that faculty contract letters would be delayed, with no additional context provided, few words of encouragement, and feeble attempts to provide clarity where there was mostly fog.

She wasn't surprised that fear and confusion had set in among many faculty members. Staff were worried, too, but tended to be more tolerant of additional work. Some faculty were known to complain about doing any *thing* that seemed in any *way* above and beyond the contracted work, protected by the ever-present specter of the collective bargaining agreement. She could practically hear the voices of specific faculty members because they said the same things so often that it was almost like reading from a script: "This is unacceptable. Someone needs to be accountable." "The lunatics are running the asylum." "We're not a widget-factory." Miriam did resent feeling personally hurt, however, since she always tried to maintain an emotional boundary between the "business" of the work and the personal aspects of the work. She frowned as she realized that she couldn't really think of any specific personal aspects of the work at the moment, even though she had been a fixture at the institution for six years before all things "pandemic" hit the fan.

At first, when the institution abruptly shut down, she had tried inviting people to "virtual office hours" with the chancellor each week for a month. When only two or three different people appeared each time, she coordinated a "pizza pick-up at the pond" event for faculty and staff, where people could come by and pick up a boxed pizza lunch and drop any concerns into an anonymous suggestions box. She was counting on a few of her leadership team members' insights to guide her decisions occasionally, but she didn't feel like she had a grasp of the socio-political landscape amidst the COVID-19 chaos, as people's levels of anxiety were rising with every news report about rising cases coupled and rumors about furloughs and lay-offs.

"What do they call them?" she asked herself. "Voluntary separations?" She sighed and glanced at the paper in front of her.

She picked up the printout of the faculty's letter of concern, passing her fingers over and across the paper, pausing as her mind rested on the thought that she actually felt grateful – grateful that the faculty hadn't posted an online petition instead. As she understood it, a few agitated faculty members had rushed to craft a letter of concern, inviting all faculty to contribute to it, and the letter grew to be 15 pages long. The contents contained items straight from the news media and ultimately didn't reflect any tangible activity that had occurred on their campus. One item that made her frown, however, was their anger about student athletics. She had agreed to allow some of the team sports to proceed, after getting input from multiple sources and conference members, and she hadn't felt good about that decision but went along with it to provide some sort of hopeful outlet for the student athletes. Now, it seemed that the decision hadn't provided the community with any solace, due to the COVID-19 outbreak that had followed, and faculty could revel in their (temporary) satisfaction at being able to shake their collective fists at the heavens.

Some of the administrators on her leadership team said that they felt "ambushed" when they learned about the letter. The athletics director got fairly defensive, saying things like: "Faculty members have no idea how hard it was to make these decisions in an unprecedented situation that no one had any previous experience trying to navigate." The new director of marketing and communications said, "It feels like I'm being tested," and "I don't understand why they wouldn't have the *decency* to pick up the phone and call me instead of doing *this*!" Miriam had worked through enough crises to understand that the communication from administration had been less than ideal, but they were facing unprecedented circumstances. The communication from faculty had been less than ideal, but they were facing extremely stressful uncertainty and felt powerless in the face of it. They didn't have the same perspective that she had and could only see part of a much bigger, more complex picture. The typical channels of communication that existed in their institutional governance structure – the joint faculty–administrator standing committees, in particular – had been eclipsed by the responsiveness demanded by this extreme situation.

In hindsight, she should have invited some faculty members to be involved in the more perfunctory ad hoc work along with the board members. Instead, the need for weekly, rather than monthly, meetings with board members blurred the lines of formality and protocol. She knew there would be damage control to be done, and that the scars would remain tender for a long time for many community members. Miriam hoped that faculty would be somewhat distracted by the work they would be doing to update their courses to meet the varied delivery modes, and that they would appreciate the hiring of several new administrators who would report to her and focus on diversity, equity, inclusion, and justice efforts. If that didn't satisfy them, she wasn't quite sure how she could do anything better. She thought about reaching out to another chancellor that she recently met during a virtual regional crisis-management forum. Before she put the letter of concern back in her briefcase, Miriam scribbled the phone number of that colleague on the paper. It was time for a friendly phone call, since she was running low on support and could use some good cheer. She paused for a moment and closed her eyes as she realized, "I feel really lonely."

How can faculty and administrators utilize governance structures to remain focused on students, who will graduate as "active participants in the world, potent advocates for human rights, confident leaders willing to take risks in the pursuit of intellectual honesty, of freedom to disagree, of justice and fairness, global citizenship, and mutual responsibility?" (Walsh, 2006, p. 4). What conditions must exist for awareness of the others' perspectives to move from understanding to collaborative action? In the sections that follow, we share insights that can inform intercultural communication in your own setting and contribute to transformation in all higher education settings – moving them from systems of authoritative control to places of "radical sharing and universal inclusion" (Mbembe, 2016, p. 45).

FACULTY MEMBER K'S PERSPECTIVE

What follows is the reaction of a composite faculty member, created by integrating reactions from focus group participants, survey respondents, and conversations with professional colleagues in higher education settings.

"Often our starting point as faculty is a distrust of administrators' motives when they're making decisions. We don't feel like we have any say. Even when we're asked for our opinions, we rarely see our opinions taken into account in the final decision. There are plenty of decisions I don't need to be part of. For example, I don't think it's my job to decide which healthcare insurance we get. Maybe there's a place for faculty input, but that's not my decision to make. Not everyone knows everything."

"But there are also plenty of decisions that faculty should be making, or at least be consulted with, as valuable sources of insight in order to come to a good decision to protect the mission of the institution. For example, when it comes to deciding what outside courses meet our own academic requirements, there are online companies that offer classes for as little as $59 a class. A decision to approve the syllabi so students can take these classes and get credit at our institution can save students thousands of dollars. But those classes are just not equivalent to what we offer or what we require in terms of academic rigor, and faculty should have input into whether or not these types of classes are acceptable to earn the degrees we confer."

"Faculty also feel like we're being managed and judged by people who don't understand what we do. There are many ways they reveal how little they know about the way we work. Administrators will ask us to basically take an inventory, as if we're counting widgets, to describe what we do and how many hours it takes. But the numbers don't always tell the full story. It gets reductionistic, and it reduces scholarly work into bean counting, and that becomes degrading for faculty. We're constantly calculating – how many points do I get for serving on this committee or that committee? Because we know that's how we'll be judged."

"During the pandemic, there was a colleague who was stressed to the point of tears and exhaustion. Her workload is more difficult compared to others because of the number of programs and students, and things kept changing as the university adjusted to the pandemic. Leadership kept throwing new tasks at us and wanted everything done immediately, and this colleague was at her wit's end. We had no say in the matter. I made a point to give her some encouragement and acknowledgment, because I could see that she was overwhelmed. Several of us reached out to see if we could take anything off her plate. I was so mad that our dean didn't think to do the same. That can make a big difference."

ADMINISTRATOR S'S PERSPECTIVE

What follows is the reaction of a composite administrator, created by integrating reactions from focus group participants, survey respondents, and conversations with professional colleagues in higher education settings.

"Things can play out differently if both leaders and faculty would just try to understand each other. When there's a controversy and faculty are angry, their first action is often to create a petition. This is a very public act that happens without any attempt to first try to resolve matters privately. I can tell you that as a president, provost, or dean, I'd prefer a phone call to a petition. A petition is horrifying...and it's a public indictment. It raises the stakes immediately and puts people on the defensive."

"When I was dean, some faculty started a petition about something. They hadn't even brought to my attention that there was an issue. I had no idea – none. If they had brought it to my attention, I would have agreed with them. But leaders also need to put more thought into how they communicate news that will be difficult. It's understandable that schools will have to cut budgets during a crisis, but leaders can be much more intentional about how they communicate and can be much more understanding of the fears involved. I had to announce some cuts in the first few months of the lockdown, and I put a lot of thought into how to convey understanding of the fear and uncertainty that everyone was feeling. I tried to be honest and open about my own limitations. I kept saying things like, 'We're going to be okay. I don't have all the answers but we're working on them. What are your questions? We'll try to figure out the answers.'"

"At least once a week, the community gets an email from me, saying essentially, 'This pandemic really sucks. I don't know what's going to happen, but I do know we'll be okay.' I think it is reassuring to people. But there are also people who distrust transparency or don't like particular decisions, so they lash out. Authenticity can help build trust. It's okay to say things are really hard right now. When we're collectively going through something difficult or painful, and we're honest about it, for a teeny tiny moment, our community gets a peak at something that helps form a relationship."

"During the pandemic and the Black Lives Matter protests, I was honest with my staff about being tired, and I shared how the events were compounded by a death in my family. I told everyone on my staff I appreciated them and named them all. It's hard to share at that level, but we need to be able to get over how hard it is. After that, I got notes of thanks for being open and for solidarity. Many leaders have no idea how to be vulnerable. They don't know it's okay. I really struggled with vulnerability when I became president. I worried that my style of leadership wouldn't be 'presidential.' I've come to learn how to be presidential in my own way."

As institutions of higher education strive to be unique communities of teaching, learning, and belonging, opportunities for shared decision-making and accountability is useful for the longer-term goal of creating a trusting community.

GOVERNANCE IN CONTEXT

Governance is a broad term that encompasses everything involved in how we run and operate our institutions of higher education – from facilities and personnel to academic programs and research priorities, from athletics and campus life to recruitment and admissions, and everything in between. Most universities attempt to use a model of shared governance, where all stakeholders participate in the decision-making to some degree.

The extent to which academic community members are included, or *feel* included, varies from institution to institution and from person to person. There are some governance structures that intentionally include students, staff, faculty, and administrators in different roles, specifically so that critical perspectives are freely shared and incorporated into planning and decision-making. In an effective shared governance model, each stakeholder group knows the expectations for their participation – the decisions under their purview. There are also systems in place to ensure that the people affected by any action are part of the decision-making process (or at least have someone representing their point of view). There is predictable vagueness that exists in some governance structures, even when the best intentions inspired the group's existence. For example, most institutions have some form of a Budget and Planning Committee (also referred to as Budget and Finance). Does each member of the committee get an equal say in how money is allocated, or do the meetings seem to exist so the Office of Finance can report out how money was spent, after the fact? Or, if a faculty member plans and executes recruiting events and wants to invite a compelling speaker who will appeal to prospective students and also wants to buy food and supplies, do they have to climb up multiple rungs of the ladder to plead for permission to receive such funding? Identifying who has access to resources and who is responsible for territory related to funding are topics that crop up often in governance meetings.

Student's Concerns

Students come to campuses seeking the full college experience, however that is imagined and/or however it has been sold to students through complex layers of marketing efforts. There are typically student government associations that meet regularly and interface with the upper administrators during some scheduled meetings throughout the academic year. Unpredictable meetings can occur due to dissatisfaction about resources, such as cafeteria offerings (e.g., are there ample allergy-friendly options?) and student activities fees, as well as perceived progress made in diversity initiatives.

Students, who are the ones who hold the power in terms of bringing tuition revenue into the institution, do not often perceive themselves as being in a position of power on committees that discuss planning and priorities. Recent research has shown that students tend to seek out faculty members rather than administrators to share their concerns (Ezarik, 2021), which has prompted some institutions to be more proactive about how they involve students in shared governance, particularly when students perceive that their safety is at risk (Person, 2021).

Faculty Members' Concerns

When it comes to academic concerns, faculty do hold much decision-making power – but not always. Topics such as assessment, course content, and plagiarism seem to fit squarely in the purview of the faculty, but what seems simple can quickly become complicated. For example, who determines the cap on the number of students in a given class? Faculty believe that they should make this decision because it directly affects the pedagogy for and quality of the learning experience. A class of ten students will be designed differently than a class of 80 students, and an ideal size depends on the subject matter, the modality, and the experience the professor plans to create. Related topics include class frequency (how many times it is offered each academic year) and how a class should be delivered (see Chapter Six for more information about online classes).

As is true for most aspects of most people's lives, if money exists in abundance and therefore isn't a serious concern, then these types of decisions are much easier. The authors of this book both remember periods during their professional careers when enrollments were strong, the U.S. economy was thriving, and therefore university budgets were robust. We were told to take chances, take risks, and "make good trouble." But at the time of this writing, those heydays of yore seem like a long time ago.

Administrators' Concerns

Every day, budget decisions are made by people who are not in the trenches, but who have purview over resources and territory that gives them that authority. For this reason, people outside of the decision-making bubble do not understand the vetting that can be involved when making decisions, and this absence of knowledge – when there is little or no clear communication – contributes to frustrations for academic community members. For example, the topic of administrative bloat (discussed in Chapter Five) – whether actual bloat or the perception of bloat – poses challenges for administrators attempting to share the governance of a large institution with multiple stakeholder groups and varying degrees of personal experience related to any particular decision being made. This is precisely why it is important to have relationships with people who can serve as guides (or metaphorical translators and/or interpreters) to provide the perspective of the "other."

Administrators must manage the increasing burden of regulations and compliance, which requires increasing numbers of staff members to complete specific tasks and to complete required reports, and more. Additionally, most institutions of higher education are committed to the ideals associated with diversity and inclusion, and this means having one or more employees with expertise to develop and implement ongoing institutional training that involves all community members, as well as a long-term budget to support meaningful change. Student athletes require trainers and, at times, physicians on hand (e.g., to mitigate concussion risks) at their frequent games. And yet another example, with regard to the chaos brought about by the global pandemic, is that institutions have had to hire additional attorneys and legal staff to manage lawsuits from students who get sick, or refunds requested for on-campus services that were reduced or discontinued during lockdown and quarantine periods.

Administrators are also cognizant of regulations that make student recruitment much more difficult than in previous decades. In the past, once students committed to a campus, other universities could no longer actively recruit them. Due to litigation that has ensued, a new ruling exists that maintains such barriers are, in effect, violations of trade agreements. So, even after students commit to an institution by paying their deposit fees, they can continue to be bombarded by other people and institutional communications – blatant attempts to "poach" students from one institution to another. As a result, institutions are compelled to spend more money on recruiting these days, just to remain competitive. As one administrator stated frankly, "If we don't have students, we don't have a school."

GOVERNANCE AS TUG-OF-WAR

When faculty and administrators envision the future of their shared institution, they likely imagine a place that embodies the values and beliefs that they hold dear. During the COVID-19 pandemic, members of these two cultural groups were forced to make some choices that would have taken so much longer in the past. All university citizens are painfully aware that the future health and sustainability of their organizations is very dependent on how institutions recuperate and bounce back from the challenges brought about by financial insecurity and related concerns that emanated from this molten center. Some academic citizens want to seize an opportunity to drop the proverbial rope in the governance tug-of-war.

One faculty participant in our research study asked, "Who gets to make those decisions? And [is there] confidence that faculty and administration can work together to make those decisions?" Another faculty member (who participated in a focus group composed of anonymous faculty and administrators) said:

> What I'm hearing from these administrators is that there is a lot of emotional intelligence here [in this focus group]. These administrators deeply care about the institutions they work for and their faculty. So we could work together. If I see that balance of IQ and EQ in their decisions, how they understand the dynamics between administration and faculty, and hear what isn't said and see what isn't obvious, I would trust them completely.

One administrator in the same focus group spoke about the challenge of conveying such trustworthiness up or down, through multiple channels of the hierarchy:

> I am just one. I have a group of administrators [who work closely with me, and] we can foster that shared caliber of EQ. But then I can be hamstrung if my VP colleagues don't share that, or if the person to whom I report at the board level doesn't share that. So that shared culture that I may be able to foster from me down, I can nurture that, but it will only go so far because I will be bumping up against something above. To advance relationships with faculty, my trust of above matters most. That's the place that the trust that

faculty want to invest in me will be believed. Otherwise, they'll say, 'She's great, but she's only going to get so far.'

This comment garnered an energetic response from a faculty member in the group:

> You brought up a good point. It's easier to foster trust when it's a smaller circle. I trust in my direct supervisor, I see this person frequently. But I don't feel like I can foster trust for the dean, president, provost. I feel like I'm just lost in this circle of people. But if my supervisor trusts those above, then I can maybe trust because someone I trust has trust in those above. Trust is built at the smaller level. When people at the top decide we'll destroy the smaller trust groups and have all the decision-making centralized, that's when trust falls apart because the person I trust is no longer part of that decision-making group at the top.

For faculty and administrators, the need for clear communication that is verifiable and consistent is important. One faculty member recalled a conversation they had had with a president once, about an issue that affects faculty members' lives. That president had replied, "Oh, that's something I wouldn't know anything about." We asked administrators in the group to share some strategies they utilize so that they can at least try to know what they don't know. "What steps can administrators take to feel confident, if not just comfortable, that they know what they need to know?

One administrator responded, saying that she surrounds herself with people who know more than she does about the things she doesn't know:

> Not being too proud or full of your position to reach out and ask for help is essential. I feel really comfortable doing that, which might be disconcerting to some people who think I *should* know. I'll have a conversation with the faculty or dean or whomever, to see if we can help each other. You don't have to go through three or four people in order to ask me a question – email me directly. Right now we're debating how to handle tuition next year. We've been using the same bad method for several years. Can we afford to charge more, do we need more revenue? I reached out to the college of business: can you and your faculty do a tuition and pricing analysis for us? They were thrilled that I'd asked them for help, and that it was inside our institution. It shows that I know I don't know everything. One thing we can do is just reach out and own that we don't

know everything. There are people who know more than you do. Find your own blind spots and find people who complement you.

SHARING IS HARD

The concept of sharing is something that we first learn about as young children, when we are encouraged to give away something we treasure, even if only briefly. Across the human lifespan, many people equate sharing something with loss, whether sharing relates to something tangible (e.g., toys, money) or abstract (e.g., ideas, power). Even on a subconscious level, the act of sharing can create some personal, internal conflict. There will always be times when some people have to make decisions and act quickly, due to a crisis or time constraints, and those may be times when decision-making cannot be shared. Sometimes, people have to make decisions that do not involve other people and constituencies. Anticipating implications for decisions, and confronting the unintended consequences of decisions, will help faculty and administrators communicate and build trust. We synthesized feedback from survey responses and comments made during focus group discussions to come up with some helpful quick practice tips:

For faculty members: it is helpful to resist the temptation to become accusatory about a decision with which you disagree. When those occasions arise, don't assume the consequences were intentional. When opportunities arise, speak up. Seek out a guide to help you understand why there was a need for such a decision. You may or may not be satisfied with the answer, and that decision may or may not actually feel justified. But the first way to learn anything new is to seek information, listen, and give yourself time to reflect.

For administrators: try to resist the temptation to become defensive about your decisions. Be candid about the fact that you sometimes have to act without the ideal level of participation from all potential groups. See how it feels to admit that there will likely be consequences that you can't anticipate. Then, invite people to make potential consequences known and assure them that it's safe to speak up and, in fact, you hope that they will.

Try – and Try Again

As we have spoken with faculty and administrators throughout our research and professional careers, common themes and threads have emerged. Faculty often cite administrators' lack of transparency, communication, and shared decision-making. Administrators tend to cite faculty members' rigidity and ability to ignore communications until they are directly impacted by a situation that they don't like. We have, however, gathered wisdom from efforts that faculty and administrators made intentional efforts to participate in shared governance.

One faculty member felt vexed because they had frequently observed impasses that occurred when administrators were perceived as cooking up their plans behind closed doors or had sought a "thumbs-up" from a small group of faculty in their circle of favorites (who never pushed back or offered a contrary opinion), and then the administrators appeared to believe that these plans either had broad faculty support or didn't need it. In order to resolve an impasse about classroom space, this faculty member invited colleagues to volunteer to invite the provost to visit their classes and experience first-hand the strengths and limitations that their space and technology resources afforded. (In some cases, "technology resources" meant having chalk for the chalkboards that were in some of the classrooms.) Almost a dozen faculty members volunteered, and the provost was willing to make the time to visit all classes at least once. As a result, the provost got to learn more about curriculum, met many students they otherwise wouldn't have encountered yet, and experienced the pedagogical choices that the faculty made, and how they could have stretched their work farther with additional resources. The group of faculty and the provost made a joint presentation to the executive committee of the board of trustees, and the provost was able to provide additional resources for departments that applied for resources from a pool of funds. Not every request was funded, but the effort was made and was sincere. It provided a reference point that faculty members could point to as a success.

One administrator was tasked by the governing board to reorganize the structure of the university – not a simple task. The chancellor created a steering committee of faculty members from across the institution and asked them to investigate options and create several models based on: (1) the institution's strongest (highest-enrolled) majors; (2) the careers that their students state they desire; and (3) data about current and future job markets and their institution's strengths. The chancellor knew very well that many faculty members would prefer to keep things as they were, so specifically and explicitly told the steering committee that maintaining the status quo was one of the possible models that they could submit for consideration. The chancellor created a process for inviting additional people into the work and for the ideas to be considered by different sets of people in different roles and offices throughout the institution. The chancellor considered it to be a thoroughly inclusive process. This was something that faculty, staff, and administrators had been saying they needed even before this chancellor was hired, so the chancellor felt pretty confident about setting the process in motion. Some people were still furious, and it was a bumpy process, but the work proceeded.

TWO CULTURES BUILDING BRIDGES

It can be difficult to change institutional practices, especially in organizational cultures that are resistant to change. In the following chapter, we explore the role that tradition plays in higher education, and how faculty and administrators can work toward establishing trust in their communities.

SUMMARY

Institutions of higher education are steeped in history and socio-political factors that are tightly woven into the fabric of any one institution, as well as the broader field of higher education. While challenges and tensions have remained consistent features of institutions over many centuries, recent research encourages academic community members, and all of human society, to identify systemic patterns that contribute to oppression and inequity that is linked to colonization. Faculty and administrators can utilize shared governance structures to proactively address such patterns, re-centering the goal of education to provide equitable access to knowledge and freedom of thought.

PRACTICE AND REFLECTION

1. Think about a time when you compromised about something in your work setting. How did you feel? What values were you most concerned about maintaining, and what felt less critical to maintain? What was the factor (or factors) that contributed to the ultimate agreement to compromise? If it felt imbalanced, what bad feelings remain that can be considered proactively, so they don't fester?
2. What are the stories that exist, or get passed down from one "generation" of institutional community members to the next? Why do you think it's so important for some people to cling to these stories? What values do these stories communicate about their identity, or the identity of the institution?
3. If you could trade places with a faculty member or administrator for one day (respectively, depending on your current role), what changes would you implement if funds and permission were not obstacles? Is there a way you could work toward these changes in your current role?

RESOURCES

Brené Brown – Dare to Lead Resources

https://daretolead.brenebrown.com

Brené Brown has become well known around the world for her work that inspires people to be courageous and to embrace their own vulnerability. This comprehensive website features a tremendous array of free materials that visitors can access, including worksheets, articles, and audio-visual materials. Whether you are in a position of leadership because of your role or because of your attitude – or both! – this website has very broad appeal and deep resources.

OpenSource Framework – Power & Equity

https://drive.google.com/file/d/1AWTFGOnGqtu074kFfasMJQ8UUrRQcSrq/view

This infographic illustrates many concepts related to power and equity, using a framework that prompts people to specifically consider resources, rules, stories, and people. This "equity approach" encourages reflection and dialogue about the differences that exist in society for people to access resources and opportunities. It provides an entry point for everyone to engage in reflection, regardless of where one is in their own anti-racism knowledge/practices.

Tug-of-War

https://www.thisgirlcan.co.uk/activities/tug-of-war/

This website features just one of many examples of activities that are healthy for body, mind, and spirit. Celebrating women and girls, the This Girl Can organization seeks to empower all women to be their healthiest authentic selves. This site can serve as a resource for anyone looking to build community within and across their institutional (or other) groups.

REFERENCES

Dobbins, M., Knill, C., & Vögtle, E.M. (2011, February 1). An analytical framework for the cross-country comparison of higher education governance. *Higher Education*, 62, 665–683. Retrieved at https://link.springer.com/article/10.1007/s10734-011-9412-4

Ezarik, M. (2021, February 24). Do students feel heard on campus? *Inside Higher Ed*. Retrieved at https://www.insidehighered.com/news/2021/02/24/do-college-students-feel-heard-professors-and-administrators-their-campuses

Mbembe, A.J. (2016). Decolonizing the university: New directions. *Arts & Humanities in Higher Education*, 15(1), 29–45.

Paradeise, C., Reale, E., & Goastellec, G. (2009). A comparative approach to higher education reforms in Western European countries. In E. Reale, I.

Bleikle, E. Ferlie, & C. Paradeise (Eds.), *University governance: Western European comparative perspectives* (pp. 197–226). Springer.

Person, S. (2021, April 11). SA aims to uplift international students' voices with committee. *The Daily Orange.* Retrieved at http://dailyorange.com/2021/04/student-association-international-student-concerns-committee/

Shattock, M. (2006). *Managing good governance in higher education.* McGraw-Hill Education.

Walsh, D.C. (2006). *Trustworthy leadership: Can we be the leaders we need our students to become?* Fetzer Institute.

Zaman, K. (2016). Quality guidelines for good governance in higher education across the globe. *Pacific Science Review B: Humanities and Social Sciences, 1,* 1–7.

Chapter Eight
Cultural Priority: Tradition

When ideas for our research first began to crystallize, we found the cultural aspects of the worlds that administrators and faculty inhabit to be very apt as we wrestled with our evolving understandings of the tensions in higher education. As mentioned at the beginning of this book, we then were able to apply a travel analogy as we considered specific elements related to culture (e.g., currency, language, ambassadors, un/intentional transgressions). Most international travelers take it for granted that they will encounter people from one or more cultural groups, who will have traditions that likely differ from their own. For example, a business traveler attempting to form new partnerships will go out of their way to learn everything they can about how to demonstrate respect to their potential new partners and, perhaps even more important, will learn as much as possible about how to avoid inadvertent words or deeds that can communicate disrespect.

In higher education, many academic practices are deeply rooted in almost 1,000 years of tradition (as discussed in Chapter Seven). The cultural history of academia is therefore biased toward practices that are linked to these origins and complicated by religious and political traditions and assumptions that have an even longer history. Researchers exploring academic culture note:

> Higher ed, perhaps more than any other industry sector, cherishes its history, traditions, ceremonies and institutional/campus culture. Those cultures can be hard to define and hard to describe, but they are harder to break from. That means taking the good and the bad, often finding back-bending ways to explain the bad.
> (Rosowsky & Hallman, 2020, par. 10)

For administrators and faculty members trying to navigate tensions in their institutions, awareness of traditions and the deep-rooted emotional and intellectual roots is critical to creating a community of trust.

THE SCIENCE OF TRADITION

While the field of psychology can boil down humans' tendency toward habits and routines to the comfort provided by predictability, traditions convey values that extend beyond simple platforms for stability. A study focused on human mobility patterns indicated that "[h]uman behavior is 93 percent predictable…regardless of the different distances people travel," ("Human Behavior," 2010). This particular team of scientists argues that although "most individuals travel only short distances and a few regularly move over hundreds of miles, they all follow a simple pattern regardless of time and distance, and they have a strong tendency to return to locations they visited before" (par. 7). Other researchers posit, however, that people uphold traditions for complex reasons: "We love tradition because of who we are as a species and how we've evolved to survive trouble" and "traditions have to include a set of certain ingredients to lodge themselves firmly in our heads and societies" (Thorpe, 2015, par. 4).

In their book *Made to Stick* (Heath & Heath, 2007), the authors propose a theory about why some ideas stick in our memories more than others – "the Velcro theory of memory." The authors reason that human memory is less like a filing cabinet and more like Velcro:

> If you look at the two sides of Velcro material, you'll see that one is covered with thousands of tiny hooks and the other is covered with thousands of tiny loops. When you press the two sides together, a huge number of hooks get snagged inside the loops, and that's what causes Velcro to seal…The more hooks an idea has, the better it will cling to memory.
>
> (p. 111)

The authors further note that "[g]reat teachers have a knack for multiplying the hooks in a particular idea" (p. 111), so it is no surprise that the culture of higher education includes a lot of traditions that are quite sticky.

As humans are living feeling beings, it is interesting to notice how some traditions evoke emotions and thoughts that strike people differently because of the lenses they wear in a given situation. In the case study that follows, we present an example of an annual tradition that brings up predictable tensions for administrators and faculty members. As you read the material, see if some of the elements are familiar to you and also make note of any new ideas and perspectives that can strengthen future interactions in your academic setting.

What types of routines are valued by people precisely because they provide the expected experience? What risks are more likely to be rewarded and

CASE STUDY: COMMENCEMENT FESTIVITIES

Ju and Max pulled up to the convention center parking lot earlier than expected – they'd purposely left plenty of time because traffic could be so terrible on graduation weekends. A security guard stopped them at the entrance by holding up the palm of his hand to them, elbow completely locked in the rigid "Stop!" gesture.

"Hey! Maybe he won't let us in and we can go have brunch somewhere!" Max joked. Ju smiled and glanced around the guard's palm to see if she could spot any open parking spaces that would provide strategic exit strategy on their way out. She noticed one of the long-time board members getting out of his Audi SUV and ruefully thought, "I wonder if he pays for parking?" The board member opened the trunk and removed a garment bag, which Ju assumed held his complimentary regalia inside.

"Graduation day is here! Weren't we just here, like a minute ago?" Max asked and crossed his eyes.

"Stop it!" Ju said, as she laughed and pinched his arm. "We're here for the students."

As they walked up the parking lot ramp, emerging into the light of day, they saw students posing for pictures with their friends and families, vendors selling balloons and roses in cellophane wrapping, and the usual downtown hubbub. This day always felt bittersweet to Ju, because she loathed sitting through the long graduation ceremonies, but she always felt happy to see students that she knew beaming with pride, joyfully participating in this academic rite of passage.

Max pointed his finger ahead of her gaze and moved his finger so she could follow his arm and notice where he was pointing: to the two reserved conference rooms – one for administrators and VIPs and one for faculty.

"There should be a sign – 'Steerage this Way' – don't you think?" Max asked, eyebrows raised. "I don't understand why they wouldn't at least *pretend* that we are all equal."

They continued walking toward the two rooms. In the first room, catering staff floated around the room, offering amuse-bouches and fizzy punch to some guests while others grazed at the continental buffet that featured colorful sliced fruit, croissants, and yogurt parfaits. Upper-level administrators were visibly schmoozing with the two celebrity speakers, board members, and other prospective donors who had been invited to the ceremony to taste what the institution was all about. Ju and Max spotted a few faculty members in the room, talking nervously with the provost. These were the anointed faculty who had been selected to participate in the processional. The president's chief of staff was chatting with the chairwoman of the board, but Ju noticed that he kept glancing at the faculty members, presumably keeping an eye on them. Maybe she was just imagining it. She wondered what political capital the powers that be were building by selecting these few faculty members – it was always an annual riddle to solve and typically bore fruit a few months later, when an announcement would be made about some new program or initiative that the faculty members were leading or developing. Always a quid pro quo.

Max opened the door to the "steerage" room, and they went inside. They stopped first at the metal clothing racks that had been wheeled in for the occasion and hung their regalia on the rack next to metal clothes hangers.

"No...*wire*...HANGERS!" Max moaned, grimacing – evoking Joan Crawford's famous line in the film *Mommie Dearest*. He did this same thing, every year. Ju always appreciated the humor. Wire or wood, she was just glad to be able to ditch their robes for a bit – it was hot and their conference room had no air conditioning. She walked over to the table with continental breakfast items and took a mini bagel and plastic-sealed cup of fruit cocktail (she liked to pick out the maraschino cherry pieces). Max made himself a cup of tea using water from the hot water airpot, and he winced after taking a sip, saying, "It always tastes like old coffee. Blecch."

Before long, the president's receptionist poked her head into the room, telling those within earshot that it was time to get lined up. Ju wondered why she didn't come fully into the room, and whether it was because she had to rush to do something else or if she didn't feel comfortable mingling with "scary" faculty members. Faculty members put on their robes, sometimes hazarding a guess about which graduate schools colleagues had attended based on the colors of the robes. Others helped people adjust their hoods and tams, some people handed out safety pins or bobby pins to colleagues, and still others used the temporary mirrors propped against the walls at 45-degree angles to make sure they looked presentable.

In the VIP room, members of the president's leadership team and board of trustees members donned their respective regalia. Most of them borrowed the regalia year to year, since they hadn't earned a terminal degree that was associated with the traditional attire. One faculty member was handed the ceremonial mace, which had been crafted from local wood and featured symbols representative of their university's region. Ju watched as the occupants of the VIP room filed out ahead of the faculty, and she could faintly hear the orchestra tuning up one floor above them.

Ju and Max stood next to each other in line and processed with the rest of the faculty, up the stairs and into the main convention hall, which was always humbling to Ju. She felt warm as parents and others applauded the faculty walking by. She saw their images being projected onto the giant screens that flanked the stage, and she both dreaded and longed to see herself up there. The VIPs were already seated on the stage as the faculty made their way to their seating area. She noted trustees, alumni, prominent community leaders – people with no direct ties to the graduating students. She sighed, feeling a tad deflated by the "make-believe" that she noticed, but that she knew other people loved, caught up in the spectacle of the ceremony.

By the end of the ceremony, Ju's cheeks hurt from smiling so much during the ceremony. She'd gotten choked up hearing the student speaker describe the sacrifices her parents had made so that she could attend college. She felt inspired to buy the book that one of the keynote speakers had written – her speech was one of the best Ju and Max could remember. As they made plans to meet up with some friends for lunch and drinks, Ju felt glad that she and Max had come together. It was hard to both love your work and feel disgusted by some of the practices and politics. But there wasn't any place else she'd rather work right now. Ju put her regalia back in the same plastic sheath she did year after year, and she knew she'd be taking it out again next year.

which ones might be deemed inappropriate if people attempt to make changes to patterns that exist because "we've always done it this way"? Institutions of higher education grapple with questions like these as administrators and faculty members bring their own perspectives to bear on situations that range from the everyday activities to the less frequent, higher-stakes events.

ADMINISTRATOR S'S PERSPECTIVE

What follows is the reaction of a composite administrator, created by integrating reactions from focus group participants, survey respondents, and conversations with professional colleagues in higher education settings.

"I love graduation, the pomp and circumstance, the festivities, the emotion…as I see students now graduating that I remember welcoming at first-year orientation. It's so heartwarming and really exhilarating at the same time."

"Graduation is really exhausting for me, I'm an introvert and it takes everything out of me….managing the constant smiling and engagement with all the trustees, the potential donors, the dignitaries, the graduates and their families….always worrying will there be some massive glitch. I am comatose for a couple days after it's all over."

"I have always had mixed feelings about honorary degrees. I remember at my first commencement as a student, a well-known actor was awarded an honorary doctorate and I felt a righteous indignation. Why would this actor be receiving an academic honor? I felt really offended. Over the years, I have been able to reduce some of my cognitive dissonance, but at core, I have never really embraced honorary degrees. It's one of the many aspects of my role that is expected for me to embrace, but I don't, not really."

"For those of us who value history and the traditions, it's jarring (and can feel disrespectful) to see graduates wear flip-flops with their robes or decorate their hats. But one time, I saw a student's hat with a message of thanks to her parents, who were immigrants. I realized I do enjoy seeing someone express their gratitude and pride at a moment of such achievement. I've come around on that one, and we've started having decorated graduation hat parties a few days before graduation."

FACULTY MEMBER K'S PERSPECTIVE

What follows is the reaction of a composite faculty member, created by integrating reactions from focus group participants, survey respondents, and conversations with professional colleagues in higher education settings.

"Graduation is technically an academic event, yet in reality, its purpose is to impress and flatter the people who have money. Faculty are the people with the closest ties to the students who are graduating on this day – serving as teachers, mentors, advisors, and friends – but we're relegated to the fringes, and for many faculty, there's no point in showing up at all."

"The provost and deans always strongly encourage faculty to attend, but they can't technically require it. When I do attend, I always have tears in my eyes from seeing the students I know, personally. I've also been the one to be invited to carry the mace and then sit on the stage with board members who have no personal connection to the graduates. But that just feels weird and awkward. It's frustrating to see people wearing a robe when they haven't earned it, or to see people receiving honorary degrees, after I worked so hard to earn mine, or to see the president acting like the speakers are now their best friends. That's the distasteful stuff that's hard to bear."

"I think the more meaningful ceremonies are the department-specific ones, or the Ph.D. hooding ceremony. Sometimes, we have smaller-scale, more personal dinners and events that we invite students and their loved ones to, leading up to the actual commencement ceremony. Those are the ones that fill your heart and feel authentic. So, much of the rest of it feels like it's just superficial fluff."

It's clear that traditions are experienced differently by people depending on their respective vantage points and connections to the inherent or implied values. The more we know about academic traditions, the more versed we can be in communicating with others who may have different perspectives and opinions.

TRADITION IN CONTEXT

Traditions have an important role in every culture – traditions help us know, embody, and perpetuate certain values. Traditions are also a way for cultures to demonstrate respect to people and the environment. Institutions of higher education are unique in that they seek to welcome people with different cultural backgrounds and beliefs into the academic community. The cultures are at times overlapping, at times clashing, and at times transformative. Thorpe (2015) explored the psychological importance of traditions for human beings and articulates three generalizations about their importance:

1. "We follow traditions because we copy people for safety" – we subconsciously adhere to some traditions because we are afraid of punishment if we choose to behave otherwise.
2. "Powerful traditions have a set of recognized elements" – the key ingredients that give a tradition sticking power are (a) a strictly defined time and place; (b) features that are repeated annually; (c) other features that vary, year to year; and (d) many symbols.
3. "Parents with fun memories of traditions have mentally healthier children" – the author notes that specific structure and positive reinforcement contribute to traditions being carried on, generation after generation (Thorpe, 2015, par. 5–12).

Thorpe also notes that traditions that involve a lot of sensory stimulation are important from a psychological standpoint. The sensory experiences tend to communicate and imprint specific significance for us. Consider the sensory elements described in the case study, such as particular food (taste/smell), music (sound), flowers/balloons (sight/smell), and regalia of different colors (sight/feel). These elements haven't accidentally continued to be included in graduation ceremonies for hundreds of years. There are intentional and subconscious reasons that commencement ceremonies look and feel similar to how they may have felt back in the 13th century, when universities were forming in select regions throughout Europe.

Pomp and Circumstance

Universities in general, and commencement ceremonies in particular, are built from centuries-old traditions that still carry significant meanings for many people. There is some variation among institutions in terms of how they organize and execute commencement ceremonies, but the traditions were important enough to academics that in 1959, the American Council on Education (ACE) tasked its Committee on Academic Costumes and Ceremonies with preparing a definitive go-to guide for such events (American Council on Education, 2020). The ceremony guide features specifications including attire, the order of speakers, and the processional flow for commencement and inauguration ceremonies.

Appearance and Aesthetics

In a recent blog post, writers at Arizona State University (2017) acknowledged the juxtaposition of ancient traditions bumping up against our modern age:

> Consider this: The leaders of an institution of knowledge march in behind someone carrying a fearsome weapon of war. Erudite faculty are led by a banner designed as a visual aid for illiterate people in battle. And everyone wears robes originally intended to keep them warm in chilly buildings in a damp climate.
>
> (par. 1)

The origins of academic dress and props, for example, date back to the 12th and 13th centuries. Researchers frequently cite a statute made at the University of Coimbra in 1321, which "required that all 'Doctors, Licentiates, and Bachelors' wear gowns" (ACE, 2020, par. 3) and note that under the rule of Henry VIII, Oxford and Cambridge initiated requirements for academic dress and empowered institutions with control over all details. Several centuries later, institutions in the United States developed their own requirements, which prompted the development of a formal code that remains in use today. In the sections that follow, we provide a brief guide that highlights some traditional items and their ceremonial significance.

Chain of Office

The chain of office, also called a livery collar, is a heavy chain/necklace or collar that is worn by the highest-ranking official at an institution of higher education. Depending on the institution, new ones may be created when new presidents or chancellors begin their terms of office. These chains originated during the Middle Ages and are representative of "the trust and authority invested in the president by a school's governing body" (Hood College, n.d.). The chain of office is typically worn only when faculty are in full regalia, such as formal academic ceremonies.

Mace

The University of Washington describes the ceremonial mace on its Office of Ceremonies webpage, stating:

> As an ancient symbol of authority, it reminds us that universities are custodians both of the enduring traditions of learning and of the power they bestow upon those who come to learn. It is also a reminder that the learning process has not always been comfortable and easy.
> (University of Washington, n.d.)

Similar to the chain of office, the ceremonial mace originated during medieval times and was used as a weapon of protection by bodyguards of high-ranking officials. Maces are used throughout the world by different governing bodies and represent official authority.

Gonfalons

A simple way of describing a gonfalon is similar to a banner or flag that represents a specific community. In the academic world, the tradition of using gonfalons emanates from medieval Italy (and the Italian word confalone). Representatives from different neighborhoods in Florence would carry their distinctive confalone when attending formal meetings, and the tradition has evolved throughout the centuries to the present time. At formal ceremonies, gonfalons are often carried to represent the different disciplines or schools that operate within an institution (Duro, 2015).

Robes

According to the ACE (2020), academic robes were originally designed with the practical purposes of: (1) keeping scholars warm, since they often studied in cold damp places, and (2) keeping books and papers dry, therefore utilizing enormous sleeves for this purpose. Over time, particularly in the late 19th and early 20th centuries, institutions established specific colors to correspond with specific academic disciplines:

- Agriculture – Maize
- Arts, Letters, Humanities – White
- Commerce, Accountancy, Business – Drab
- Dentistry – Lilac
- Economics – Copper
- Education – Light Blue
- Engineering – Orange
- Fine Arts, including Architecture – Brown
- Forestry – Russet
- Journalism – Crimson
- Law – Purple
- Library Science – Lemon
- Medicine – Green
- Music – Pink
- Nursing – Apricot
- Oratory (Speech) – Silver Gray
- Pharmacy – Olive Green
- Philosophy – Dark Blue
- Physical Education – Sage Green
- Public Administration, including Foreign Service – Peacock Blue
- Public Health – Salmon Pink
- Science – Golden Yellow
- Social Work – Citron
- Theology – Scarlet
- Veterinary Science – Gray (ACE, 2020).

If you recall the importance of territory as a cultural priority for administrators and faculty members (discussed in Chapter Six), it's not surprising to learn that scholars in different disciplines preferred to be distinct from other disciplines. These robes are typically worn during formal ceremonies that occur during an academic year, such as graduation ceremonies and others that mark the formal start of the academic year.

Convocation

One scholar reflects on the meaning of convocation as follows:

> For the academic community, the good tidings of great joy surround the welcoming activities for the incoming freshmen and/or

the capstone celebrations for the graduating seniors. To wit, it is really all about our recognition of the scholarly circle of life. One comes in, another goes out.

(Gavazzi, 2012, par. 4)

Similar to graduation ceremonies, convocations typically include faculty members in full regalia, students and family members, and administrators and board members.

Syllabus

Gannon (2016) writes, "an effective syllabus invites students into our course. It's a document that talks about possibilities rather than prohibitions. It allows students to see why they get to take our course, not why they have to" (par. 16). The word "syllabus" is traced to Latin roots, referring to a list of lectures that students will receive. Today, a syllabus can also contain institutional policies and other regulatory information that some faculty feel obscures the welcoming spirit of the document. Many faculty understand the syllabus to be a pact between students and faculty members.

In the wake of the murder of George Floyd and subsequent anti-racism efforts, more frequent conversations among faculty members across numerous disciplines have occurred. Many faculty are committed to ongoing efforts to decolonize syllabi in their courses and more broadly in their institutions. Such work includes explicitly demonstrating how a particular discipline and institution has benefited from (and perpetuates) colonization. One faculty participant in our research study shared her struggle to expand resources in her course syllabus beyond those that upheld the traditional theories, predominantly authored by European White male scholars. Her primary challenge was identifying Indigenous resources – oral histories or vital ways of knowing – that hadn't been published in "mainstream" academic journals. She realized how hard it can be to change systems that are immutable. The work involves more than simply checking items off of a checklist or tucking in Indigenous resources among numerous others. A helpful article is Tuck and Yang's (2012) *Decolonization is not a Metaphor*, which has inspired additional comment and critique.

Tassels

Tassels have been used for centuries to serve many purposes, ranging from the decorative to the military to indicate completion of formal education. When students graduate from a post-secondary degree program, their tassels indicate that they have completed the requirements for their particular program. The symbolic turning of the tassel, typically from right to left, symbolizes the transition from degree candidate to graduate.

Diplomas

The original sheepskin diploma "originated in the Middle Ages, when traveling scholars used to haul it around as proof of their education" (Sawyer, 1979, par. 7). In more modern times, paper or parchment diplomas came to replace animal materials. The value of a diploma varies from graduate to graduate, since proof of education can now be verified with a click of a mouse. While not everyone wants to invest in the cost of framing something that will hang on a wall, for so many students and families, diplomas represent tremendous effort, investment, and human potential.

Students' Concerns

As if the cost of a higher education program wasn't enough, there are frequently additional high costs associated with the numerous traditional activities that students are encouraged to attend. "The cost is significant; caps and gowns for rent can cost around $100 and much more to buy" (Strauss, 2017). In her article about academic attire, Strauss cites one particular institution's regalia order form, with items that range in price from a tassel for $10 to a "Masters Set" for $145.95. A "Stole of Gratitude" costs $39.95, and while a lovely gesture to provide a thank-you to someone who's made a significant impact along someone's academic journey, a thank-you note is also very effective and much less expensive. Students frequently note their confusion about numerous events and officials, such as what a convocation is and why they are required to attend, or who a provost is and what they do. With the frequent changes that typically occur in administrative leadership, students sometimes make no overt attempt to pay attention to the ceremonial details. They just follow instructions without understanding the rationale or tradition, and they don't feel strong connections with the officials as they do with the faculty.

Faculty Members' Concerns

Faculty members attained their positions after completing an average of 7–10 years of academic study. They may have identified an interest in their undergraduate study that grew into a passion that propelled them into Master's and doctoral programs, accordingly. As their interests evolved into specialized expertise, they likely engaged in deep, sustained research advancing that particular specialty in ways other academics had not considered. Scholars earn their robes and hoods and celebrate that accomplishment with a hooding ceremony that carries great meaning on levels both personal and professional.

For these fundamental reasons, something like the awarding of honorary degrees is not just a formality to members of the faculty culture. Depending on the recipients, it can feel outright offensive, especially when honorary degrees are awarded to "cronies" of the administration (e.g., prospective donors, board members). Some faculty acknowledge that it feels like cultural appropriation, a topic that has recently gained renewed attention in research and public discourse. Cultural appropriation is generally understood as a dominant group exploiting the culture of a less privileged group, and race and ethnicity have been historically linked to the practice (Nittle, 2021). When someone (who may not perceive the gesture as significant) is selected as an honorary degree recipient by administrators and board members in positions of power, and then handed a title and attire that faculty members worked very hard to attain, members of the less powerful cultural group may resent the ceremonial practice. They likely also resent those who made the decision.

Administrators' Concerns

Administrators tend to view traditional activities as vital to their institution's stability. They report balancing the competing demands of governing board members and graduates' family members and everyone in-between. They feel responsible for the perceived success of every event in the cycle of an academic year, from convocation through graduation and alumni weekends, and the fiscal stability of their institution is always at the forefront of their minds.

Some administrators fret about every detail of a specific tradition and seek input and support from administrative staff to execute the many layers involved in an event or annual activity. These administrators understand that the order of the processional march at commencement, for example, can carry unintended implications and feel to long-standing community members to be a dramatic change to beloved traditions. In this example, the cultural humility demonstrated by upper administrators can go a long way in avoiding unnecessary tensions and communicating respect to staff and faculty members.

It is predictable that members of institutions of higher education communities will occasionally make changes to traditional materials and practices, and these traditions have likely been set and observed as treasured rituals at each individual institution for many years. Changes are therefore not made or received lightly.

IMMUNITY TO CHANGE

Considering how entrenched and interdependent academic traditions may be, academic community members will be most successful when they are intentional about contemplating change. We have experienced first-hand the difference that it makes when administrators make tangible efforts, for example, to learn how one change may affect or alter other aspects of the wider academic ecosystem. The term "immunity to change" is one that people have experienced, if not named, within their academic institution, when they perceive people to be fundamentally resistant to any sort of change, big or small.

Authors Kegan and Lahey (2009) authored a book with this precise title, anchoring their work in the premise that "the endless parade of professional development programs, personal-improvement plans, leadership trainings, performance reviews, and executive coaching reflections a deep-seated optimism among leaders" (p. 2) about change within their organization. The authors quickly follow this statement, however, with the revelation – almost a confession – that when they have engaged leaders in honest conversations about their institutional investiture in developing human resources, there is "a deep-seated private pessimism" (p. 3) that leaders acquire over time, as they realize that people and places are not easily changed.

Considering the research conducted by Northeastern University scientists noted earlier in this chapter, which found that human behavior is 93% predictable (2010), a significant amount of time and resources can be saved. As institutions of higher education attempt to respond to new and increasing challenges and opportunities, rather than follow the predictable patterns of investiture in superficial efforts, they would be better served making time and effort to invest in the "learning life" of their institutions. This involves developing engaging institutional community members in practices that promote intercultural communication and understanding the identities that contribute to a group's cultural ties to traditions.

TRADITION AND IDENTITY

It's hard to let go of something that is part of our identity, and we are protective of the identities we claim for ourselves. When we engaged focus group participants – administrators and faculty members – in discussion about their institutional traditions, some of the comments revealed much about their perceptions about institutional identity and values.

For example, one administrator said, "There's a disconnect between the faculty culture, which focuses on the intrinsic value of education, and other cultures that tend to view education as an extrinsic value." Another administrator opined:

Knowledge, enlightenment, perspective, balance, diversity—those are things that a college education provides people that they might not get on another route. It's so important that we have historical perspective on the systems we're living with today. If all we see is the system as it exists today, with no idea of how it was created and why, or of who's working for the good and why it matters. There are so many things that are valuable [about college]. We need to raise the conversation of value above workforce development. We want to be part of that, but so many other things are above that line. We get lost sometimes.

A faculty member shared their feeling that faculty members "are administrative functionaries without a clear mission because the traditional mission of higher education has been taken over by profiteering – we sell an experience, but we aren't even sure what the experience is."

Another faculty member contributed their observation: "There's a fear of becoming run like a corporation, treading on all the traditions and prior understandings that academia embraces, instead of a university. We are being sold out, sold down the river, sold to the highest bidder."

Even as administrators may attempt to learn about traditional practices that imply or convey values to students and community members, they often find themselves frustrated and their efforts ultimately thwarted when they meet with enormous resistance. Administrators often attempt to initiate changes that they believe – based on their understanding and consultation with other stakeholders – will improve effectiveness, productivity, and quality, and perhaps will save money or increase revenue. Yet despite these efforts, they can meet with pushback that falls under the "immunity to change" umbrella.

That's Not Who We Are

The following examples, shared by research group participants, illustrate the resistance that can exist in spite of administrators' efforts and intentions.

A new dean joined a university that didn't give students letter grades. Instead, professors were required to prepare narrative assessments. The goal was to develop, rather than judge, a student's progress. One by-product of his institutional practice was that faculty reportedly felt that they were "drowning in the workload." First, the assessments themselves took much longer than grading papers or scoring tests. In addition, when students applied to graduate programs and they didn't have letter grades or quantitative GPAs indicated on their transcripts, faculty members often had to assign conventional letter grade equivalents anyway, accompanied by lengthy letters of recommendation that translated the students' talents and potential into sharable soundbites. The faculty complained constantly and bitterly about the workload, but responded viciously when the new dean suggested that they change the grading model. Some faculty members accused him of bringing too much change to their school without thorough consultation.

In another example, a space utilization committee recommended to the chancellor that a prime location currently being provided at no cost to a local non-profit organization could be better utilized for student outreach services. Aware that the non-profit organization had used this space for many years, and that any change could have negative community relations impact, the chancellor asked his team to first assess potential impact. They discussed the situation with key community members versed in the history of the arrangement. After careful consultation and assurance that there would be no problem if the university offered the alternate space (also at no cost), the chancellor approved the plan. The community relations director informed the chief operations officer at the non-profit organization, and within 24 hours, the chancellor was facing public outrage over the decision.

Clearly, there are some traditions that exist because time has made the practices and relationships precious. In other cases, some traditions are toxic and yet continue to exist at a systemic level – woven into an ideology or legacy – well beyond the boundaries of any one institution. In the section that follows, we briefly address such "traditions" of exclusion and discrimination, which are themselves the subject of many articles and books. Our intent is to mention these as examples of practices that exist, not because they are cherished or comfortable for all institutional constituents, but because we hope that these examples prompt more extensive reflection and investigation that leads to transformation.

TRADITIONS OF EXCLUSION

Some traditions we have described in this chapter are troublesome in that they may seem annoying and frustrating. Other traditions, such as the exclusion of women and Black, Indigenous, and People of Color (BIPOC) in university enrollment and hiring practices, are examples of traditions that are disturbing and legally and psychologically dangerous.

Women in Academia

The American Association of University Women (AAUW) was founded in 1881, "when a small group of female college graduates banded together to open the doors for women's career advancement and to encourage more women to pursue higher education" (AAUW, n.d., par. 1). Since its founding, the organization has grown to include over 170,000 members and has contributed reports that directly influence current academic policies and practices, as well as federal legislation. Imagine how steep the climb was when this organization published one of its first reports – "an 1885 paper disproving a prevailing myth that college impairs a woman's fertility" (par. 3).

Research continues to focus on women's roles in academic leadership (e.g., Bornstein, 2007) and discrepancies in salaries and promotion opportunities (e.g., Bartels et al., 2021). Researchers, such as Ballenger (2010), identify cultural and structural barriers that exist in higher education and propose strategies that include mentoring, professional development opportunities and resources, and close examination of promotion and career advancement practices.

BIPOC Community Members in Academia

Similarly, the exclusion of BIPOC faculty and administrators is another tradition that has been challenged strongly and publicly – historically and more recently. Laws have mandated and enforced racial, ethnic, and religious segregation from many public and private institutions throughout the history of higher education in the United States. This is what prompted members of Black communities in the 1800s to establish universities – Historically Black Colleges and Universities (HBCUs) – built on the belief that everyone deserves access to higher education.

Some research into the influence of race and ethnicity on faculty and administrators (e.g., Sulé, 2011; Walkington, 2017) utilizes critical race feminism (CRF), which derives from critical race theory (CRT), and includes feminist theory as well as intersectionality (see Crenshaw, 1989). Much of the research notes the value of diversity, demonstrating how it positively affects civic engagement, intellectual engagement, and interactions among community members, including problem-solving skills and critical thinking. In practice, however, research notes ugly realities related to stereotypes, "tokenism," and aggressive behaviors that are experienced by employees as well as students. As members of institutional communities, it is imperative that administrators and faculty members engage in collective efforts to examine practices that perpetuate systemic oppression and sustain barriers to opportunities. As mentioned throughout this book, these systems are not operating in isolation from political, social, and historical factors that influence society. They are deeply entrenched and interconnected with traditions in higher education and as such are very difficult to change.

We propose that this is a vital challenge. Traditions of exclusion are not the kind of traditions that compassionate people cling to with nostalgia. Our responsibility is to identify and explore why these traditions persist: why enrollment and hiring of traditionally excluded groups still doesn't match the enrollment and hiring of groups with more traditional privilege. How might we be contributing to and perpetuating these traditions? How might our own actions or opinions be affecting individuals with whom we have conflict?

TRADITION AND TRANSFORMATION

Tradition and transformation are parts of the broader subject of social progress. People in parts of the United States are engaged in difficult discussions related to statues, buildings, and street names that honor people from centuries past, who supported (and/or fought and died for) the institution of slavery. Others are engaged in heated discussions about identity – who gets to decide what pronouns someone can use to identify themselves, and are others required to respect those decisions in educational settings (see Flaherty, 2021)?

This topic has immediate and direct, practical applications for our work in classroom settings, and institutions of higher education are full of traditions that impact community members directly and indirectly. The annual graduation ceremony is a very obvious and visible tradition, but certainly not the only place where cherished rituals bump up against modern ideas. When institutions identify challenges that confront any members of that community, their efforts are greatly aided when a foundation of trust exists. When trust is present, the work can commence with confidence that while the path through complicated terrain may be difficult, the results will be worth the effort.

SUMMARY

Institutions of higher education are anchored in centuries of history and traditions that perpetuate the values of the time. Researchers have explored the concept of traditions through disciplinary lenses that include psychology, whereby they identify elements such as predictability in human behavior and tendencies to return to past practices. Such awareness can help administrators and faculty members understand why it is often difficult to get anyone to change when they perceive that something they value is at risk. As institutions consider traditions, it is important to commit to efforts that include eradicating traditions and practices that perpetuate systems of oppression and exclusion if a community of trust can ever exist with integrity.

PRACTICE AND REFLECTION

1. What alliances exist in your institution that reflect a shared vision for an inclusive, respectful community? How are these visible, supported, and/or challenged? What resources and communication strategies provide opportunities for these alliances to meet the needs of all community members in a predictable, protected way?
2. Think about a ceremonial event in which you participated at your institution in the past few years. What were the roles that were evident in terms of prestige and power, and who decided who was in these roles? What, if any, aspects of the event made you uncomfortable, even angry, and how did you process those feelings and/or communicate with others about what you were thinking and feeling?
3. Everyone in an academic institution has the potential to be a leader and change-maker and to create new traditions that complement existing ones. A community may even decide to end some traditions to make space for new ones that uplift people and behaviors that have been excluded in the past. If you had unlimited time and resources, what new tradition would you design? Who would you engage in this effort, and how do you think your effort would be received by administrators and faculty, respectively?

RESOURCES

Rethinking Schools

https://rethinkingschools.org/

Rethinking Schools is a non-profit advocacy organization that has as its core mission "sustaining and strengthening public education through social justice teaching and education activism." The website features resources and archives on myriad topics, as well as publications that can be used to advance personal and professional growth and learning.

Smithsonian Institution Archives' Collection – Primary Sources

https://siarchives.si.edu/

The primary sources available here lend visual, tangible support to historical events and belief systems that contribute to many of the traditions in existence in the United States today. As you explore the archives, you'll find many, many topics to explore, which branch off into new directions, and you can also explore the different museums, galleries, and zoo that are all part of the total Smithsonian offerings.

Malcolm Gladwell's 'Revisionist History' Podcast – Higher Education

https://www.pushkin.fm/show/revisionist-history/

Author Malcolm Gladwell is known for his many columns in *The New Yorker* and many books, such as *The Tipping Point*. In his podcast episodes, Gladwell focuses on "something from the past – an event, a person, an idea, even a song – and asks whether we got it right the first time." In a three-part mini-series, Gladwell examines access and affordability (*Carlos Doesn't Remember*), spending priorities *(Food Fight)*, and philanthropy and accountability *(My Little Hundred Million)*. Gladwell received both praise and harsh criticism for his portrayal of some traditional practices and belief systems in higher education.

REFERENCES

American Association of University Women. (n.d.). *Our history* [Web site]. Retrieved at https://www.aauw.org/about/history/

American Council on Education. (2020). *Academic ceremony guide*. https://www.acenet.edu/Programs-Services/Pages/Academic-Ceremony-Guide.aspx

Arizona State University. (2017, May 7). Medieval times: The history and the meaning behind the regalia of ASU's commencement. *Arizona State University*. https://arizona-state-university.medium.com/medieval-times-the-history-and-the-meaning-behind-the-regalia-of-asus-commencement-bb5973064df4

Ballenger, J. (2010). Women's access to higher education leadership: Cultural and structural barriers. *Forum on Public Policy Online, 5*, 1–20.

Bartels, L.K., Weissinger, S.E., O'Brien, S.E., Ball, J.C., Cobb, P.D., Harris, J., Morgan, S.M., Love, E., Moody, S.B., & Feldmann, M.L. (2021). Developing a system to support the advancement of women in higher education. *The Journal of Faculty Development, 35*(1), 34–42.

Bornstein, R. (2007). Why women make good college presidents. *Presidency, 10*(2), 20–23.

Crenshaw, K. (1989). Demarginalizing the intersection of race and sex: A Black feminist critique of antidiscrimination docrtrine, feminist theory and antiracist politics. *The University of Chicago Legal Forum, 140*, 139–167.

Duro, A.J. (2015, June 14). *The gonfalon: A brief history*. Retrieved at http://www.accentbanner.com/blog/the-gonfalon-a-brief-history

Flaherty, C. (2021, March 29). 'A hotly contested issue.' *Inside Higher Ed.* Retrieved at https://www.insidehighered.com/news/2021/03/29/court-sides-professor-who-repeatedly-misgendered-trans-student

Gannon, K. (2016, October 28). What goes into a syllabus. *The Chronicle of Higher Education,* 63(9), A40.

Gavazzi, S.M. (2012, August 23). The true meaning of convocation. *HuffPost.* Retrieved at https://www.huffpost.com/entry/the-true-meaning-of-convocation_b_1821893

Heath, C., & Heath, D. (2007). *Made to stick: Why some ideas survive and others die.* Random House.

Hood College (n.d.). *Chain of Office.* https://www.hood.edu/discover/about-college/history/chain-office

Human behavior is 93% predictable, research shows. (2010, February 19). Northeastern University College of Science. Retrieved June 12, 2021 from https://cos.northeastern.edu/news/human-behavior-is-93-predictable-research-shows/

Kegan, R., & Lahey, L.L. (2009). *Immunity to change: How to overcome it and unlock potential in yourself and your organization.* Harvard Business Press.

Nittle, N.K. (2021, February 4). A guide to understanding and avoiding cultural appropriation. *ThoughtCo.* Retrieved at https://www.thoughtco.com/cultural-appropriation-and-why-iits-wrong-2834561

Rosowsky, D.V., & Hallman, K. (2020, May 20). Communicating culture in a distributed world. *Inside Higher Ed.* Retrieved at https://www.insidehighered.com/views/2020/05/26/importance-culture-binding-higher-ed-institution-together-during-crises-pandemic

Sawyer, K. (1979, June 16). That old sheepskin nowadays probably isn't-baa. *The Washington Post.* Retrieved at https://www.washingtonpost.com/archive/local/1979/06/16/that-old-sheepskin-nowadays-probably-isnt-baa/292864eb-0b9a-4b16-90c5-3954d2c8009a/

Strauss, V. (2017, May 20). Why caps and gowns at graduation? Let's go back 900 years. *The Washington Post.* Retrieved at https://www.washingtonpost.com/news/answer-sheet/wp/2017/05/20/why-caps-and-gowns-at-graduation-lets-go-back-900-years/

Sulé, V.T. (2011). Restructuring the master's tools: Black female and Latina faculty navigating and contributing in classrooms through oppositional positions. *Equity and Excellence in Education,* 44(2), 169–187.

Thorpe, J.R. (2015, December 23). Why we love traditions, according to science. *Bustle.* Retrieved at https://www.bustle.com/articles/131377-why-we-love-traditions-according-to-science

Tuck, E., & Yang, K.W. (2012). Decolonization is not a metaphor. *Decolonization: Indigeneity, Education & Society,* 1(1), 1–40.

University of Washington. (n.d.). *Office of Ceremonies*. Retrieved at https://www.washington.edu/ceremony/tradition/symbols-meanings/university-mace/

Walkington, L. (2017). How far have we really come? Black women faculty and graduate students' experiences in higher education. *Humboldt Journal of Social Relations: Special Issue – Diversity & Social Justice in Higher Education, 39,* 51–65.

Part Three

Two Cultures, One Community

Chapter Nine

Cultural Imperative: Trust

In a recent article in *The Chronicle of Higher Education*, the author advises, "As my dad always says, human beings are unpredictable. Thus, when someone reacts poorly or makes an uncharacteristic mistake, it is important to take a moment to look at the whole picture" (O'Grady, 2021, p. 61). It's striking to note the perception that humans are unpredictable, when scientific research points to the exact opposite phenomenon (see "Human Behavior," 2010). Perhaps human behavior is predictable in its unpredictability. One thing that we have learned over decades of work in higher education is that tensions between faculty and administrators are predictable – that much we know. How these tensions are manifested in different institutions of higher education make them therefore common – by virtue of their very existence – as well as unique, due to the institution's interconnected and evolving culture, history, and environment.

When trust exists in this midst of the predictable unpredictability, concerns of faculty members may be perceived as less antagonistic, and administrators' decision-making authority may be perceived as less threatening to the natural order of the institution. Some researchers have acknowledged the complexity in understanding the life of institutions of higher education, noting that studies have often "been dominated by debates on the problems and benefits of globalization, marketization, managerialism, and academic capitalism" without "paying attention to another main organizing principle of higher education institutions: their cultural dimensions. What is actually happening in the internal life of the higher education institutions, and how can we study the topic from a cultural perspective?" (Välimaa & Ylijoki, 2008, p. 1). No one can deny the challenges that have impacted higher education (discussed in Chapter Three) during the last several decades, involving structural changes, fluctuating economic factors, and socio-political forces. We believe that this book provides a starting point and foundation for institutional discourse, which acknowledges these factors as perceived and processed through the cultural lenses of faculty and administrators who, in turn, impact the experiences of the other.

IN _____ WE TRUST

When you read the heading above, you likely filled it in yourself, perhaps with one of the following words: Mom, God, Snoopy. Filling in the blank with each of those words opens opportunities for associations such as a hug, a dollar bill, or a warm blanket, and each of those images provides comfort in its own way, depending on the individual and the moment in time. (The etymology of "trust" is actually linked to the German word "trost," which means "comfort.") Institutions of higher education provide additional variations on the theme of trust, primarily in the "organizational culture" that is promoted through institutional "mission, environment, leadership, strategy, information, and socialization" (Välimaa & Ylijoki, 2008, p. 2).

Others suggest that establishing trust is further complicated because people tend to think of trust in three distinct ways:

1. Strategic trust – the trust employees have in administrators to make strategic decisions related to mission and vision, resources, and intelligence
2. Personal trust – ways in which employees are fair to each other and consider others' needs in addition to their own
3. Organizational trust – the trust employees have in the institution, its systems and processes, and follow-through on promises (Galford & Drapeau, 2003).

These types of trust are interconnected and impact productivity and effectiveness.

The notion of trust as something distinct and rational is, we argue, less accurate than an understanding of trust as something co-constructed through relationships and discourse. This socio-cultural construct of trust is what can support and/or inhibit institutions' attempts to be innovative, and faculty and administrators consistently note trust as a primary, shared value and goal.

Trust Detours

In order for institutions to build and sustain trust, community members must be able to recognize it and even the absence of it.

> The hiddenness and personal nature of trust can be a problem for relationships, teams or organizations. How can you fix something that is not expressed or shared? How do you even know that trust is lost? Paradoxically, there must be at least a little trust in order to discuss its lack and make attempts to rebuild it, while if the loss of trust remains unaddressed, the relationship will grow more and more distant.
>
> (Jaffe, 2018, par. 7)

Faculty and administrators regularly encounter opportunities to communicate about trust in many ways, ranging from lower-stakes conversations about a new font that will be used on the university website to higher-stakes discussions about commitments to hire more Black, Indigenous, and People of Color (BIPOC) staff and faculty in the next two years. It is quite common, however, for:

> decisions perceived to have significant consequences for people's lives [to be] widely distributed across a number of 'gatekeepers' within the education structure. Within the university context, individual instructors, student services personnel, and administrators each make decisions that can have important consequences for both students and colleagues.
>
> (Denisova-Schmidt, 2020, p. 248)

At many institutions, particularly large institutions, a considerable number of critical functions (e.g., teaching, administrative support tasks, research) are routinely conducted without any communication, visibility, or awareness between and among constituents. In the absence of information that affirms expectations or alleviates anxiety in multiple directions, it is not uncommon for misunderstandings to develop and for these to fester into more toxic distrust. If faculty members' and administrators' experiences with each other routinely lack authentic exchange, the absence of the communication then becomes the validation for the wariness that faculty or administrators experience with the other.

Corruption

When distrust exists over prolonged periods, misperceptions and disagreements can sometimes be perceived as unethical behavior. This has been a frequent subject of research in recent years, due to the many challenges currently facing institutions of higher education. It is fascinating to think

TWO CULTURES, ONE COMMUNITY

CASE STUDY: CUTTING-EDGE CONSORTIUM

Members of the community logged into the virtual meeting space, rectangle by rectangle, popping up and changing the configuration on Jai's screen rapidly. They turned off their camera and took another bite of the sandwich they'd been trying to eat for over an hour. The number of institutional meetings had truly multiplied – they couldn't be imagining it – since the virtual meeting technology had been adopted at their institution. At least they were able to multi-task during meetings – check email, text with colleagues, eat lunch...

"Thanks for coming, everyone!" Jai flinched instinctively as the VP of Advancement's rectangle suddenly filled their entire screen. Jai quickly switched to a different mode so they could see 20 or so rectangles at a time, instead of just the speaker's giant visage.

"We're thrilled to be able to announce the names of people whose proposals have been accepted for the first-ever *'Cutting-edge Consortium!'* Can I see some 'jazz hands' in the room?" The VP of Advancement held his hands up near his ears, palms facing the camera, and then moved them to and fro in a flurry, smiling broadly. The motion was copied by numerous members of the virtual meeting space.

"Razzle-dazzle, y'all!" thought Jai, disgustedly. They were not surprised by how eager some people were to please the higher-ups, at least visibly.

The VP of Advancement described how excited he was to be able to shepherd several projects through this very competitive, first-of-its-kind, cutting-edge process – from concept to implementation – thanks to funding that had been generously donated by several board members and others. Jai wondered how many board members had actually donated funds, and how much, and what the conditions were that convinced them to write their checks. Jai knew that no faculty members had been involved in the design of this new initiative. Although Jai caught themself thinking the word "new," noting wryly that "anything called 'cutting-edge' now is already behind the times." Their attention drifted off...

"Congratulations, Jai!" The VP of Advancement was smiling and razzle-dazzling on screen. Jai smiled back, feeling a bit stunned and confused, trying not to look as caught off-guard as they were. They hadn't thought for a minute that their proposal was going to be approved. Friends started texting Jai messages of congratulations and silly GIFs. Jai was cautiously excited, but noticed a tiny, prickly pang of suspicion about what they were getting into – what the next steps would be, and how all of this would play out.

Next steps played out quickly. That afternoon, Jai received an email from the grants office, inviting them to a meeting with the dean the next day, to discuss plans for the implementation of the proposed work: pop-up art spaces for high school students throughout the neighboring city. Jai imagined these would be open-access, safe spaces where students could take a break, play with an assortment of art materials to express their feelings, worries, and ideas (anonymously), and where they could access information about health and wellness resources in the community. In the email, the grants officer wrote that Jai should come to the meeting with their budget proposal and plans.

Jai went over the proposal line by line, looking for any places that seemed thin, and thinking of any possible questions they might encounter from the grants officer and dean. They felt excited about the possibility of this project really taking off, as they'd been developing the idea for over a year and a half, and yet they still felt a bit uneasy, and didn't sleep soundly that night, for no perceptible reason.

The next morning, Jai logged into the virtual meeting, and was greeted by the dean while they awaited the grants officer.

"Congrats, Jai – this is really exciting!" the dean said, though his voice didn't seem to match the level of excitement of his spoken words. Jai thanked him for his letter of support, and then the grants officer joined them, apologizing for her lateness, having just come from another virtual meeting with the president and a donor.

"So, first let me say congratulations again, Jai! Your proposal was really well-received, and we're so excited to get this project up and running." The grants officer continued, sharing details about what the timeline would be, how much money Jai would be allocated from the pooled funds, and what percentage the university would receive for overhead to manage the grant. After several minutes of talking, the grants officer asked Jai if they had any questions.

"Um, yeah," Jai said slowly. "I'm just not clear about the university's 'cut' part. What are those funds for, exactly?" Jai tried to look at their expression on their computer screen, hoping that their face didn't reveal any emotion.

"Overhead. It's just overhead," the grants officer said matter-of-factly. "With any grants, there's always overhead expenses factored into the budget." She looked at the camera directly, awaiting any follow-up.

"Oh, OK. I see," said Jai. "I didn't realize that these were 'grants.' I thought these were donations from the donors the VP of Advancement mentioned yesterday – board members and so on." Jai could feel themself starting to sweat. "I guess I just want to make sure that the funds are used so that the students get the most they can from the funds. That's all."

The grants officer assured Jai that their work would be "fabulous" and that the concept was "cutting-edge" and then excused herself to transition into another meeting. Jai was left with the dean, and Jai blinked their eyes, feeling quite cartoon-like, during the few moments of awkward silence that occurred before the dean filled the space.

"Don't worry, Jai. We'll make sure that you get what you need for this project. It's really exciting. Do you have any questions?"

Jai scrunched up their nose and mouth for a second, paused to look up at the ceiling, and then asked, "What happened to the budget proposal that I submitted, which I thought was approved? I don't understand what 'overhead' there is, when this is something I'm executing, that's occurring off-campus, and it's not a workload thing."

The dean paused for a moment, clearly trying to think of how to say what he was going to say. "Let's just say that I brought up these exact points, and ummm not sure that I can really do anything about it. I can help you try to tweak your budget so it is within the parameters. There would be an adverse reaction if you push this. It's complicated."

"An adverse reaction??" Jai blurted out, trying not to laugh. "What does that even mean?" Jai shook their head, incredulously, and the dean just stared back at Jai, not offering any words to confirm or deny Jai's suspicions.

"OK, then," Jai said. "Whatever. Just let me know what the bottom line is, and I'll decide whether or not I can do it or need to walk away."

As they each logged off of the meeting, Jai felt a familiar stomach ache starting to percolate. Jai picked up their phone and texted their work friend, Ian: "I have icky news."

about how the absence of trust, especially distrust, impacts all members of an academic community.

Denisova-Schmidt (2020) explains that sometimes issues emerge because "individuals do not understand ethical lines or realize they are crossing them" and sometimes "behaviors may have become so ingrained that participants may no longer think of them as corrupt" (p. 248). For example, the author notes that students may neglect to cite a source in a research paper because they don't have a grasp on the rules about citing the work of others in a literature review. Once they learn the skills, they can avoid those errors. Similarly, "the inability of a university to account for all of its funds may signal financial impropriety, or it may only reflect shortcomings of poorly trained accountants" (Denisova-Schmidt, 2020, pp. 249–250). When trust exists in an institution, the impulse to assume ill intent for some personal gain is curbed by the faith that someone has the best intentions underlying their behavior, and an appreciation for humans as predictable in their unpredictability prevails.

What opportunities for communication were missed in the example above? How could any of the people involved have shared information that would have informed others of their perspective and contributed to better understanding and subsequent action? When you consider the intentions of all of the people involved, were these intentions at odds, aligned, or is it hard to determine?

FACULTY MEMBER K'S PERSPECTIVE

What follows is the reaction of a composite faculty member, created by integrating reactions from focus group participants, survey respondents, and conversations with professional colleagues in higher education settings.

"It is hard to feel trust in individuals with no proven track record supporting faculty members in any substantial way. Each time there's a change in leadership, the new person comes in wanting to make their mark. Sometimes, the president will bring in people from their previous institutions, and then faculty are automatically suspicious. It's not fair, I know, but many faculty have been burned so many times that they've lost their trust of administrators in general, especially when they come from outside of the academic world."

"One time an administrator was hired in a temporary role, and people liked her a lot because she seemed to be less concerned with looking good and more committed to doing good. I think she was in a 'sweet spot,' where she didn't have to prove anything to anybody, and knew she'd be gone in a year, so she could forgo some of the political stuff and focus on getting things done, forming relationships…She's the second best administrator I've worked with in almost 30 years. She knew more about faculty and what we do in three weeks than the former administrator knew in three years."

"I don't understand why administrators can't get out of [faculty's] way and let us do what we know is best for students and the institution. We wouldn't be here for decades if we didn't love what we do. They put so many barriers between us and resources, it's ridiculous. If they can't trust us to be responsible with resources, then why are we here?"

ADMINISTRATOR S'S PERSPECTIVE

What follows is the reaction of a composite administrator, created by integrating reactions from focus group participants, survey respondents, and conversations with professional colleagues in higher education settings.

"Faculty act as if we're purposely withholding information, but there are some times that we can't share everything about a situation, for reasons that are delicate. Sometimes I have to say 'I don't know' when I actually do know, and other times I feel uncomfortable when I don't know the answer to a question and my not knowing puts a target on my back."

"There's pressure on all sides, so there's not often an easy way through even simple decisions like a coffee cart ice cream machine purchase. You have no idea. And I don't really have a community that I can go to and share my frustrations, because people would wonder what was 'really' going on if I ever singled out a faculty member to have lunch or coffee. The few times I've invited people for coffee were met with a really lack-luster response. After a while it's not worth the effort because there's so little tangible return."

"My hope is that I can be trusted over time once people learn that we are not on opposite teams. I hear people say that there's a culture of fear and people are afraid of losing their jobs if they speak up, but I can't imagine that that's really so pervasive among faculty. There's no reason that people shouldn't feel safe with me. Some people say it's a climate problem, but I think it's a culture problem."

It is commonly said that trust isn't something that is given – it's something that is earned. In the sections that follow, we present information that helps illustrate how communication and other actions contribute to a solid foundation of trust. This requires consistent practices and elements that foster trust among offices, individuals, and across cultural groups within the institutional community.

TRUST IN CONTEXT

When the subject of "trust in the workplace" is used as a search term, most of the material that comes up is related to the world of business and to globalization as a universal objective for those in the world of business. As mentioned throughout this book, institutions of higher education straddle several "worlds," primarily education and business. It's therefore not surprising that education leaders turn to business literature to guide their behavior. In a recent article for *Forbes* magazine, Jaffe (2018) highlights six qualities that he argues are fundamental to the existence of trust in an individual or organization:

1. Reliability and dependability – behavior that demonstrates that a person/organization is true to their word and lives up to their commitments
2. Transparency – clear, thorough communication as opposed to an absence of information that breeds anxiety
3. Competency – behavior/evidence that demonstrates that a person/organization is qualified and capable of meeting expectations
4. Sincerity, Authenticity, and Congruency – words/behavior that align with what a person/organization proposes to say/do; consistent and non-contradictory words/actions
5. Fairness – all people and all sides of an issue/organization are considered
6. Openness and Vulnerability – person/organization is able to accept responsibility in times of prosperity and difficult times; humility and vulnerability are modeled and acceptable (Jaffe, 2018)

These qualities are relevant in an academic community, as in all communities. Some additional examples of ways that faculty and administrators grapple with authentic trust are related to having difficult conversations and developing a greater capacity for self-awareness and emotional regulation (Gunsalus et al., 2019). Numerous faculty members shared (with the authors of this book) stories about instances when they felt bullied by someone within their department and, in spite of meetings with human resources personnel or administrators, nothing happened to the bully and the individual therefore felt more vulnerable for coming forward in the first place, and distrusting of the support systems in their institution. Administrators shared stories about feeling attacked by faculty members during meetings, and if angry feelings were expressed by faculty, then any response administrators gave, that even hinted of an angry tone, was perceived as outrageous and inappropriate behavior.

Some researchers assert that "issues of risk underpin the fundamental tensions within the notion and practice of trust in the educational setting. Those who are trusted acquire a freedom that can be abused" (Curzon-Hobson, 2002, p. 266). In an examination of the relationships in higher learning environments, Curzon-Hobson argues that the higher learning setting "is characterised by a transforming, dialogical learning environment" (p. 266) that helps groups to raise questions and engage in learning that results in "understanding of their interrelationships in the world"

(p. 266). This resonates with some principles of intercultural communication theory discussed in Chapter One, in that it is the interaction that is necessary for the transformation of the cultural groups involved. Depending on the perspectives held by members of different groups within the institution, a different stance toward risk-taking and vulnerability can encourage and impede intercultural communication.

Students' Concerns

Students enter an academic institution with expectations about learning and other experiences, and they have typically come through a pre-K-12 educational experience in which they were in positions of being told what to do, instead of what they "get to do." Many students form trusting relationships with faculty members with whom they share a passion about a discipline, a poet, or a pastime. For many faculty members, students' enthusiasm for a subject refuels their own passion reserves, and therefore, a mutually rewarding learning experience can develop where learning for learning's sake is the priority, and power dynamics about grading are not the primary force in the learning relationship.

When students trust their faculty members, they are apt to share information about themselves and their friends, to seek assistance with academic and sometimes personal challenges, and to seek guidance about career options. Students do not tend to have these close relationships with administrators, most often due to the frequent turnovers in senior leadership positions and the infrequent opportunities for informal interactions among faculty and administrators. Some students are called out for accomplishments related to athletics (e.g., breaking a sports record) or diversity, equity, inclusion, and justice (DEIJ) leadership (e.g., joint task forces), but they report feeling skeptical about these types of honorific occasions, which feel less sincere than their relationships with faculty and mentors.

Faculty Members' Concerns

Faculty members, anchored most often in one primary discipline, have established specific skills that allow them to tell stories from these academic perspectives. In higher education settings, they are able to weave together understanding with students and colleagues whose own unique perspectives contribute to knowledge that is interpreted and influenced by time and cultural factors. Their own higher education experiences taught them to trust the scientific method, to question and challenge absolutes, and to recognize their own biases and positionality in research.

It is not as easy, however, for faculty to be objective when it comes to cultural priorities, such as resources, territory, governance, and tradition. When faculty members see themselves as change agents and ambassadors for the institution, with expertise that complements that of administrators, the relationship shifts into one that opens possibilities.

Administrators' Concerns

Administrators know that the more they can demonstrate commitment and support through their work, they will garner more trust for their academic institution (Cohen, 2015). Some administrators develop stronger relationships with faculty and staff because of trust that reflects a "social exchange." In practice, this is evident in examples such as more positive dispositions when employees feel valued, or uncertainty about the competitive higher education landscape prompting a competitive spirit "enhancing an organization's long-term success and survival" (p. 51).

In larger institutions, trust is also important for administrators whose supervision and responsibilities are distributed, due to logistical and organizational realities. Administrators are aware that their priorities must be consistently conveyed and upheld, and they sometimes struggle to have systems of accountability in place that ensure that their communications and priorities are, in fact, carried out accurately and effectively. This requires what Cohen (2015) notes as "interdependence, and people must therefore depend on others in various ways to accomplish their personal and organizational goals" (p. 52).

As new challenges are encountered by the higher education community, faculty and administrators are most successful as partners who will learn, make mistakes, and continue to strive to achieve their potential together. The sections that follow provide a brief introduction to topics that are explored in greater detail in Chapter Ten. We intentionally use the notion of "practice" here for two reasons: (1) to contribute to your capacity to understand the perspectives of others, and (2) to remind ourselves that we are always learning and growing, developing skills and knowledge that we strengthen each day in our respective roles.

PRACTICE LISTENING

In the article referenced at the beginning of this chapter, O'Grady (2021) advises academic community members to strive for "fewer accusations, less defensiveness, and more listening. We need to avoid going into a conversation angry. We need to respect how others process information or events. Finally, we need to put empathy at the forefront of every conversation"

(p. 62). As noted previously, faculty and administrators in our research study expressed challenges having difficult conversations. Wherever humans exist, conflict will naturally arise, and therefore it benefits any institution to practice listening and open channels for communication. When faculty and administrators practice listening to each other, they develop muscle that will support their increased capacity to navigate challenging situations.

O'Grady provides concrete conversation starters that provide the speaker with a subsequent opportunity for active listening, and each of the following may be helpful in numerous higher education scenarios (e.g., when someone gets visibly upset during a meeting, when someone has been accused of wrongdoing by another colleague, when someone is demanding more information or explanation for a decision that has been made):

- We need to discuss what happened, and it may be difficult, but I want you to know this incident does not reflect the person you are, and it's not going to define you."
- "I want to address the situation, but first, I'd like you to tell me your side and how you're feeling. It may help me better understand where you're coming from."
- "We both understand the situation could have been handled better, and we need to discuss strategies to ensure this doesn't happen in the future. But first, I want to take a few minutes to understand why you reacted that way."
- "OK, I respect that you don't want to talk about this right now. Why don't you take some time to reflect upon what happened, and we can talk later this week? It's important to me that we discuss this, but I understand you may need a little time to digest." (p. 62)

It is important to reiterate that trust is an evolving dynamic – not an endpoint or destination. As such, trust can change from a state of fragility to one of resilience depending on different times and relationships. Authors note that the loss of trust takes a toll on an institution financially, as well as psychologically, and for that reason, it is vital "to remember that trust is an ongoing exchange between people and is not static. Trust can be earned. It can be lost. And it can be regained" (Jaffee, 2018, par. 15).

Repair

In his book, *The Developing Mind* (2020), Daniel Siegel proposes an understanding of the concept of "the mind" as one that is distinct from the brain and therefore influenced by relationships and exchanges that we have with others. In this sense, listening becomes a powerful tool in repairing perceptions and establishing new patterns for communication. In an interview ("Interview with", n.d.), Siegel describes the mind as "patterns in the flow of energy and information...as well as how energy and information flow between brains or among brains, as in a family" (par. 7). This echoes the critical dynamic that we have repeatedly emphasized as important in intercultural communication – the transformative relationship of one entity with another.

Siegel also articulates the importance of relationships, which impact our social and emotional development. It is in the everyday exchanges between people that communication becomes more than simple talking – Siegel proposes that contingent communication (par. 23) is how we take in signals from others, make sense of them, and send back signals. Other terms for the transformative give-and-take include "reflective dialogue" and "collaborative communication" (par. 27). Each of these terms represents the type of listening that enhances opportunities for people to talk "about thoughts, feelings, perceptions, memories, sensations, attitudes, beliefs, and intentions" (par. 28). It's this precise dynamic that is reflected at the core of intercultural communication and what contributes to a deeper understanding of self and others.

PRACTICE INCLUSIVE LEADERSHIP

That word "inclusion" is used widely to reflect different values and priorities. It is also a term that can convey confusing messages about priorities, depending on how the message is delivered and by whom. In institutions of higher education, with regard to leadership and building trust among employees:

> [i]nclusive leaders are those who are people-oriented, understanding, and passionate, and are more socially savvy than procedure heavy. They inspire change, take the time to understand the jobs of those they manage, and are committed to the team's emotional well-being. They are ride-or-die for their employees, and put the needs of others before their own. They actively listen more than talk, and ponder more than react.
>
> (O'Grady, 2021, p. 62)

On a fundamental level, "inclusion happens when you value both the differences and the commonalities of the others" (Jain, 2018, p. 208). Examples of how this may be manifested in higher education settings include a provost inviting faculty members to serve on a search committee for a new Chief Financial Officer, faculty members seeking a dean's input as they prepare materials for an accreditation visit, and faculty and administrators collaborating on a theme for the graduation celebration that will bring together students, families, and alumni. But having everyone at the table is not sufficient, there must also be genuine engagement and inclusion of the input of the other in decision-making and implementation.

In their recent research, Jain (2018) proposes a model for practicing inclusive leadership, containing the elements of empowerment, accountability, courage, and humility (EACH). The elements are summarized as follows:

Empowerment – converting a situation where communication is blocked into a situation where communicators are free and able to transfer thoughts freely, without hesitation

Accountability – holding one's self and others responsible for inclusive communication; using your voice

Courage – having the willingness and ability to engage across differences; stepping outside of one's comfort zone to consider things from another perspective

Humility – taking the opportunity to reflect and think about how we can learn, understand, and accept our mistakes and learn from others; this involves listening. (pp. 208–211)

Every one of these elements has been discussed in this book and in decades of research in higher education communities, and the definitions of these terms will likely resonate with faculty and administrators. During periods of relative calm and stability, these elements can be articulated, practiced, and reflected upon. The COVID-19 crisis challenged all faculty and administrators to call upon resources – material and emotional – and prompted the study of inclusive leadership during times of crisis.

Some validating findings emerged from a research study that models communication across disciplines and contexts, as the researchers engaged participants in Wuhan, China – a city now etched in the minds of everyone who has experienced crisis related to the global pandemic. The researchers conclude that employees "tend to appreciate a leader who is open and available and recognizes the employees' anxiety caused by perceived or actual threats. The leader's attitude and behaviors tend to be contagious and serve to reduce stress" (p. 10). Furthermore, the authors recommend that "leaders should focus on providing, as much as practical, a psychologically and physiologically safe environment" (p. 10). In spite of the best intentions, it may not be possible for every effort to be successful, or for every message to land well among community members. It is therefore also important for institutions to develop skills in practicing compassion – for self and others.

PRACTICE COMPASSION

The practice of compassion for self and others is associated with one of the primary tools that helps people reduce stress, and that is the ability to be present in the moment. In higher education, it is difficult to be in the moment when so many aspects of work involve planning ahead: scheduling classes a semester ahead of the current one; projecting enrollment numbers for the next fiscal year; developing strategic plans for ten or more years.

Experts have identified shifting conditions and characteristics that that are currently influencing the lives of students, faculty, staff, and administrators within the academic community:

- Excessive competition
- Misalignment of teaching and research
- Disproportionate rewards
- Injustice in working environments
- Concentration of power with insufficient checks and balances (Denisova-Schmidt, 2020, p. 250).

Denisova-Schmidt also notes that universities with a tradition of shared governance are now struggling with the cultural adjustment resulting from administrative decisions being consolidated among a smaller group of decision makers. All of these factors contribute to the difficulty anyone may have staying in the present moment and stretching one's awareness to consider the perspectives of others when the stress responses wired into our human body and brain are engaged.

Cultivating our capacity to focus on the present moment and turn attention inward – away from the myriad distractions and concerns – invites us "to overcome, at *any age*, the limitations and blind spots of current ways of making meaning" (Kegan & Lahey, 2009, p. 6).

To develop a greater facility with being open to other ideas and perspectives, and potential faculty–administrator collaborations, activities related to generating gratitude and noticing interconnectedness are quite useful. In the following, final chapter of this book, we provide concrete exercises to help you practice increasing your awareness – of your body, breath, being, and more.

Adopting an intercultural perspective contributes to empathy, compassion, and increased awareness of the diversity of roles and expertise that exists in institutions of higher education. These factors contribute to the level of trust that exists in the community. Administrators know that faculty highly value autonomy and the ability to control many aspects of their work. Faculty members know that administrators strive to serve the good of the whole, which means that they may have to juggle competing interests and priorities. As distinct cultural groups within the broader context of an institutional community, each culture potentially disables members' awareness of alternative social realities (Del Favero & Bray, 2005, p. 56). Faculty and administrators will establish trust when they develop the capacity to understand the perspective of the other and turn that understanding into action.

SUMMARY

Trust in higher education is a topic of much interest across different disciplines, such as business and psychology, and some challenges defining trust relate to the various ways that trust exists and is perceived by community members. The absence of communication and regular sharing of information can negatively impact relationships when these deficiencies come to be viewed as corruption – of an individual or the institution as a whole. Intentional practices in terms of listening, inclusive leadership, and compassion contribute to the overall health and wellbeing of faculty and administrators, particularly when trust is tested during times of crisis.

PRACTICE AND REFLECTION

1. Think about a time when you have experienced comfort in your academic environment. Did your level of comfort parallel the trust that you felt for a supervisor, or the institution as a whole? If so, what concrete experiences contributed to that sense of comfort. If not, what concrete experiences obstructed the establishment of trust between colleagues?
2. How many words does it take for you to communicate with someone close to you that you want a glass of water? That you are trying to decide between a few vacation destinations? That you need some help filling out your tax return? Are there short-cuts or patterns that have grown over time, which reduce the necessary words in order to convey the same meaning? How can you establish shared meaning with people whose perspectives are less familiar to you, and for whom your style of communicating is less familiar?
3. Consider a time when the institution was thrust into an emergency situation and resources were allocated by an administrator without broad input or lengthy discussion. How was the decision received by faculty and/or administrators? What ideas do you have for different steps that could help in a future time-sensitive situation?

RESOURCES

United Nations – Department of Global Communications

https://www.un.org/en/department-global-communications/building-partnerships

The United Nations has had decades of practice establishing practices that honor differences, respect multiple perspectives, and open channels for dialogue about many issues around the world. This website provides examples of collaborative efforts that engage global community members, in the hope of advancing critical priorities. What lessons can be gained from reading about specific efforts and initiatives?

Children's Library Lady

https://childrenslibrarylady.com/books-about-honesty/

This website is a wonderful resource for children's books on more topics that one can imagine. This particular page features an assortment of books written by a diverse set of authors, which explore the theme of trust and honesty through funny, poignant, and provocative stories. You'll recognize some classics and make some new discoveries. All of these titles are equally enjoyable when shared with others.

Headspace

https://www.headspace.com/

This website is a rich resource for articles and activities related to mindfulness and stress-reduction. Visitors can browse materials that cover a broad range of topics, including meditation, sleep, and procrastination. There are also resources that focus on interpersonal topics, such as "What happens when we dislike someone," that lend themselves well to reducing workplace tensions.

REFERENCES

Cohen, A. (2015). *Fairness in the Workplace.* Palgrave.

Curzon-Hobson, A. (2002, August 6). A pedagogy of trust in higher learning. *Teaching in Higher Education: Critical Perspectives, 7,* 265–276.

Del Favero, M., & Bray, N. (2005). The faculty-administrator relationship: Partners in prospective governance? *Scholar-Practitioner Quarterly, 3*(1), 53–72.

Denisova-Schmidt, E. (2020, June 11). *Corruption in higher education: Global challenges AND Responses*. Brill|Sense.

Galford, R.M., & Drapeau, A.S. (2003, February). The enemies of trust. *Harvard Business Review*. Retrieved at https://hbr.org/2003/02/the-enemies-of-trust

Gunsalus, C.K., Luckman, E.A., Burbules, N.C., & Easter, R.A. (2019, January 10). Fostering trust in academic departments. *Inside Higher Ed*. Retrieved at https://www.insidehighered.com/advice/2019/01/10/why-trust-crucial-academe-and-what-you-can-do-cultivate-it-opinion

Human behavior is 93% predictable, research shows. (2010, February 19). Northeastern University College of Science. Retrieved June 12, 2021 from https://cos.northeastern.edu/news/human-behavior-is-93-predictable-research-shows/

Interview with Daniel Siegel, MD. (n.d.). *MentalHelp.net: An American Addiction Centers Resource*. Retrieved at https://www.mentalhelp.net/blogs/interview-with-daniel-siegel-md/

Jaffe, D. (2018, December 5). The essential importance of trust: How to build it or restore it. *Forbes*. Retrieved at https://www.forbes.com/sites/dennisjaffe/2018/12/05/the-essential-importance-of-trust-how-to-build-it-or-restore-it/?sh=1875d4464fe5

Jain, N. (2018, December). Inclusive leadership and effective communication: An unbreakable bond. *Language in India, 18*(12), 207–216.

Kegan, R., & Lahey, L.L. (2009). *Immunity to change*. Harvard Business Press.

O'Grady, K. (2021, March 19). How to manage through emotional exhaustion: Those of us in academic leadership are not talking enough about mental health. *The Chronicle of Higher Education, 67*(14), 61–63.

Siegel, D.J. (2020). *The developing mind: How relationships and the brain interact to shape who we are* (3rd ed.). The Guilford Press.

Välimaa, J., & Ylijoki, O. (2008). *Cultural perspectives on higher education*. Springer.

Chapter Ten
Beyond Theory: A Plan for Action

The tensions that exist between administrators and faculty members in higher education are as predictable as any other human conflicts and have been examined and described in research literature through the lenses of various disciplines, including economics, education, philosophy, and psychology. The conundrums have also inspired satire – in cartoons for *The New Yorker*, such as Sipress's (2009) "Daddy works in a magical, faraway land called Academia," and novels such as our (the authors') shared personal favorite, *Straight Man*, by Richard Russo (1997). As the protagonist in *Straight Man* observes a dilemma in which members of his academic community are stuck in a particular situation, he expresses understanding borne out of a new sense of clarity and compassion that comes from lived experience:

> Clearly, the only solution was for all of us to take one step backward so that the door could be pulled open. By this point a group of plumbers, a group of bricklayers, a group of hookers, a group of chimpanzees would have figured this out. But the room contained, unfortunately, a group of academics, and we couldn't quite believe what had happened to us.
>
> (Russo, 1997, p. 391)

It is challenging for a group of tenacious, intelligent individuals embodying different perspectives, backgrounds, and dispositions to come to consensus on many things, to be sure. Yet, there is a fundamental itch to learn new things that inspires so many people to enter into careers in academia. Therefore, the challenges are tightly woven into the fabric of the work and the worlds that administrators and faculty members inhabit, reinforcing the existence of tensions as new learning and new challenges are encountered.

This chapter presents information curated through the lens of intercultural communication and is intended to prompt reflection and action in academic communities. We hope that the process will contribute to shifts in impasses that continue to plague members of institutions of higher education. When administrators and faculty members learn to collaborate, to believe that vulnerability and humility are not weaknesses but opportunities for connection, and engage in discourse that contributes to practices of listening, inclusive leadership, and compassion, then systems built from a position of trust can rest on foundations that grow stronger and deeper over time.

ENVIRONMENTAL TOXINS: RESILIENCE AND RISKS

Researchers in human development validate the experience that positive outcomes can arise in spite of adversity. The concept of resilience is referred to by Masten (2014) as "ordinary magic," meaning that ordinary experiences and processes contribute to humans' abilities to thrive. We think it is responsible and vitally important, however, to state that there are some situations that are so unhealthy – to mind, body, and/or spirit – that it is better for people to choose a new environment. We recognize that this is easier said than done, and that such a decision entails interrelated complexities (e.g., relationships, career plans, financial considerations).

The surveys we received from administrators and faculty members, and focus groups we conducted with participants representing distinct and mixed groups, provided evidence of environmental challenges that reinforced headlines in academic literature and vice-versa. In the past five years alone, articles published in academic media outlets have included the following headlines and excerpts:

- A President's Suicide (Seltzer, 2016)

"Presidents can feel isolated…[t]hey don't have peers on campus. Trustees are their employers. Vice presidents work for them" (par. 11).

- Aftermath of a Professor's Suicide (Flaherty, 2017)

The carefree academic way of life (if it ever existed) has been replaced by new funding pressures, increased administrative work, the decline of the tenure track and a more corporate, consumer-driven model of education. And while student mental-health issues have received much attention and destigmatization in recent years, it's unclear how much of that has translated to the professoriate, where there's a premium on clarity of thought (par. 12).

- How One Leader Set a Toxic Tone, Spurning Allies She Needed Most (Stripling, 2017)

...continued presence at the helm makes fund raising a needless struggle. Her clashes with the institute's Faculty Senate and its student union, and her dismissals of numerous high-ranking officials who had enjoyed broad support on campus, have irrevocably strained relations with some prospective donors (par. 19).

- *Toxic Friday: Resources for Addressing Faculty Bullying in Higher Education* (Sabina, 2021).

"While more resources are now in place to support academic bullying and hazing, new faculty must be vigilant in identifying potential toxic workplaces in which their career ambitions might be thwarted or disrupted" (par. 8).

- *Can Higher Ed Save Itself? Business as Usual Won't Solve the Existential Challenges We Face. Will Anything?* (Paquette, 2021)

"Only an obtuse observer could deny the ailing state of America's universities. Our maladies are legion, and are easily diagnosed: exploding student debt, decreased state investment, the decline of the college graduate income premium, and disruptive demographic shifts" (p. 32).

Given the range of subtle and severe threats that are present in institutions of higher education, it is a testament to the resilience and imagination of so many individuals, over centuries of practice, who have been able to re-imagine education objectives and spaces. It is this very intellectual capacity, which strengthens these types of reform and revision efforts, that also allows people to envision an alternative path and an exit from their careers in higher education.

Adaptation and Exit

To some professionals, changing jobs or leaving the field of higher education may seem like giving up or a sign of weakness. We argue that if an administrator or faculty member determines that a higher education environment is not healthy or ideal for oneself, this is actually very astute. Such awareness illustrates Sternberg's (2019) definition of adaptive intelligence in the fullest sense – including "the narrow sense of changing oneself to fit the environment...[and] the broad sense of additionally changing the environment to fit oneself and selecting new environments as necessary" (Sternberg, 2019, p. 4). In his writings over several decades, Sternberg has adapted his theory of intelligence as the field of psychology has been influenced by time and knowledge contributed by scholars in the field. Sternberg, somewhat playfully, acknowledges that adaptation of humans and cockroaches has been influenced by culture and context (although cockroaches have been adapting in a more limited sense for approximately 300 million years).

We encourage everyone to reflect on the "fit" that they experience in their own institutions, roles, and lives. If the negative aspects of the workplace are more toxic than fulfilling, and more threatening than invigorating, then we strongly recommend seeking advice from colleagues and mentors outside of the academic environment. Later in this chapter, we provide some suggested resources as a starting point for such exploration.

In the sections that follow, we revisit the overarching goal of building trust between administrators and faculty members. The sections echo some topic areas in Chapter Nine focused on developing skills through practice – practicing listening, practicing inclusive leadership, and practicing compassion.

These exercises and resources have been developed and selected to complement the work that was presented in the previous chapters. For example, as you read and experience the materials in the following sections, consider again the case studies in Chapters Five through Nine, which feature scenes and perspectives of administrators, faculty members, and others. Each case study is specific, introducing a common disagreement or misunderstanding, and yet broad enough to create opportunities to explore administrator and faculty cultural groups in more detail, and dig down into why individuals feel so strongly about certain decisions or feel like a cultural priority is being threatened by particular actions (Figure 10.1):

- Resources – we want to be valued
- Territory – we want to be seen
- Governance – we want to be heard
- Tradition – we want to be respected

In spite of perennial challenges, the "university is also a vitally important social institution" (Ginsberg, 2013, p. 201) and "a bastion of relatively free expression and, hence, one of the few places where new ideas can be discussed and sharpened" (p. 202). The sections below are anchored in this spirit and will stretch and reinforce your own thinking as you promote greater intercultural communication in your academic community.

PRACTICE LISTENING

The following materials have been curated to provide examples of action and inspiration that will contribute to deeper listening and mutually beneficial connections with others. The skills that develop through listening experiences

BEYOND THEORY: A PLAN FOR ACTION

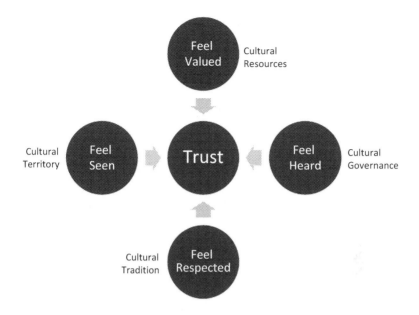

Figure 10.1 Cultural priorities and trust.

are applicable in myriad workplace situations and foster new ways of encountering people with opinions and experiences that differ from your own.

Activities

Listening – Inside and Out

Materials needed: none, although pencil and paper are needed if reflection is included at the end.

This activity is designed for one person or a group of people, and individual or group reflection can follow. Depending on the group and the setting, this activity serves as a starting point for engaging in a series of reflections and discussions that can strengthen awareness of connection with others. In preparation for the activity, you may want to record yourself speaking the instructions that follow using a phone or other recording device, so that you can listen to the instructions rather than read them.

1. Begin by finding a comfortable place to sit – in a chair, on the floor, or on a bed or couch. We recommend sitting up with your back against the chair, wall, or cushion, with your feet resting flat on the floor (as opposed to dangling and potentially distracting you by calling your attention to finding a resting position for them).

2. Close your eyes, or find a resting place for your gaze on a place across from you, and bring your attention to your breathing. Notice how you breathe – in and out – and how your chest or stomach rises and falls with each breath, in and out. Continue this for a minute or two, paying attention to your breathing...in and out...in and out...
3. When you notice your thoughts moving away from your breath and your body, gently remind yourself to return to your breathing.
4. After a few minutes, intentionally bring your awareness of the sounds occurring outside of your immediate space. As sounds from outside come to your awareness, see what you notice – patterns of sounds, one after the other; loudness or softness; beginnings and endings. Continue listening to and noticing these sounds for a few minutes.
5. When you notice your thoughts moving away from your awareness of outside sounds, gently remind yourself to return to listening.
6. Bring your attention to your breathing again, and to what you notice in your body and about the boundaries of your body – how your back is resting against the chair/wall/cushion, and how your feet feel against the ground. Notice how your breathing engages your body, inside and outside.
7. Next, notice the interplay with the inside and outside – how your listening influences your breathing, your attention, and what you feel. With each breath, notice your connectedness to yourself and the world.
8. When you open your eyes, or return your focus to the present moment, notice the sights and sounds and feelings that you experience after this exercise. If you want to reflect, take a few moments to jot down what comes up for you – where did your mind wander? What sounds did you notice? What feelings did you feel, and where in your body did those feelings reside (head, neck, shoulders, stomach)?

Drawing Duos

Materials needed: chart paper or other large paper; markers or crayons; index cards with words or photos of familiar objects on them (e.g., butterfly, skyscraper, clown). If using images, these can be cut from magazines or printed out in advance.

This activity is designed for small groups of people, who will divide into pairs. The instructions are simple:

1. One person in each pair will draw first, and the other will give instructions. The person giving instructions will tell the artist what

to draw based on the word/image on the index card that they draw from the pile of cards.
2. The activity begins with time on a clock or watch – two minutes – and the instruction givers begin telling the artists clues about what to draw, without explicitly naming what the object is. For example, if the image on the card is a butterfly, the person giving the instructions might say,

> You're going to draw something that is symmetrical. If you divide it in half, the two sides would be the same, reflecting the same shape left and right. Start with a straight line that is the middle. Draw a circle at the top. Next, draw two small lines that come out of the circle.

And the instructions can continue from there, and vary accordingly.
3. When the time is up, the artists can compare their drawings to the words/images on the cards, and if they are unfamiliar with the item, then they can ask questions about what the item is, it's purpose, it's typical location, and more. Then, the participants switch roles.
4. When each member of the pair has taken a turn, the pairs – or the whole group – can discuss what it felt like to be in the two roles. What might have been helpful in terms of communication and language? What felt intimidating in terms of following orders under pressure? This activity is helpful in identifying roles and responsibilities, as well as assumptions about language and understanding.

Word Play

Materials needed: an object that can be passed or tossed to other participants (e.g., small/soft ball, flower, stuffed animal, rock).

This activity is designed for a group of people, ideally 12–20, although it is possible for larger groups to divide into smaller groups and for small groups to find the exercise useful. If possible, the group should sit in a circle – in chairs or on the floor, as is comfortable.

1. To start the activity, one person says a word and tosses or hands the object to another participant. For example, a person says "ice cream" and passes a flower to a person sitting two seats to their right.
2. The person receiving the object then defines the word (e.g., "a sweet, delicious cold treat that I love in the summertime"). That person then thinks of a different word and passes the object to another member of the group.

3. Depending on the members of the group, the words that come up for people can range from simple and concrete to more abstract and potentially uncomfortable (e.g., "art," "justice," "spirit").
4. As a group, discuss the experience, and whether or not there were words that felt more or less comfortable or challenging to define, for various reasons. You can decide in advance whether the group wants to include a "pass" option for anyone who feels puzzled or anxious about responding in the moment. After, it is also helpful to note any sense of judgment that may have inhibited participants during the activity. How does listening to and with each other help shift expectations for communication with each other in your setting?

Digital Media

A Bit of Optimism Podcast – Extreme Listening

https://www.listennotes.com/podcasts/a-bit-of-optimism/extreme-listening-with-w_ihxr8LH-P/

In this episode, Simon Sinek features documentary filmmaker Deeya Khan, whose film *White Right: Meeting the Enemy* is noted below. What makes this episode so relevant is the manner in which Deeya Khan is able to listen to the words and ideas of men who, before getting to know her through their conversations, would have supported the continued racist practices that compelled her to make her documentary in the first place. This podcast explores the concept of deep, authentic listening that leads to transformative thinking and stronger relationships.

StoryCorps

https://storycorps.org/

StoryCorps is an organization committed to preserving and sharing "humanity's stories in order to build connections between people and create a more just and compassionate world." This site features resources that encourage conversations among people and also hosts an archive of many, many stories that have been recorded between individuals on a range of topics. Visitors to the site can explore and listen to countless exchanges that are humorous, poignant, and inspiring.

Why It's Worth Listening to People You Disagree With

https://www.ted.com/talks/zachary_r_wood_why_it_s_worth_listening_to_people_you_disagree_with

In this TED talk, speaker Zachary R. Wood shares ideas about why it is important to listen to people whose ideas don't necessarily align with our own and may not be the kinds of ideas we want to hear. He describes how we can build empathy and be stronger, not weaker, when we acknowledge alternative perspectives. The benefits of opening one's self up to ideas that challenge our own can have an immediate impact on relationships and trust.

Additional Resources

The Art of Dialogue

https://spectrum.mit.edu/winter-2001/the-art-of-dialogue/

This MIT Spectrum newsletter features the words and ideas of William Isaacs, co-founder of MIT's Organizational Learning Center. Isaacs describes the significance of dialogue in helping to solve problems in "a multicultural, global society" and how listening is critical to thinking and talking together to shift the relationship of power.

Difficult Dialogues Initiative at Clark University

https://www2.clarku.edu/difficultdialogues/pdfs/DD-keynote.pdf

This transcript is from a specific talk given by Diana Chapman Walsh, whose wisdom is also shared below in a context related to compassion. In this address, she specifically focuses on the importance of dialogue and asks how we can "take some risks and break down some of the barriers that perpetuate...isolation, polarization, suspicion, and mistrust" that create obstacles to meaningful, transformative exchange.

The Pedagogy of Listening (Rinaldi, 2001)

https://static1.squarespace.com/static/526fe9aee4b0c53fa3c845e0/t/540fce31e4b00c94d884e002/1410321969279/Pedagody+of+Listening+-+Rinaldi+-+Fall+2001.pdf

This article has become a beloved classic piece that educators return to and use as inspiration in the field of education. Carlina Rinaldi is revered around the world for the work that she has done in early childhood education – pedagogy and practice – anchored in Reggio Emilia, Italy. Rinaldi describes listening as more than a verb that means "hearing" with one's ears. She describes an active stance that expands to include one's values, beliefs, and stance as an educator in relation to others. The definitions and examples provided in this piece can serve as a helpful guide for adults working with people of any age.

PRACTICE INCLUSIVE LEADERSHIP

The following items have been selected to provide tangible examples of inclusion that extend beyond a superficial definition that simply means more people in a shared space. Inclusion is more effective when the perspectives and strengths of others are integrated into the environment, and ego or personal gain takes a back seat to the greater good of the institution. We are confident that leaders exist in every pocket of an institution of higher education, and that trusting relationships lay the groundwork for individual institutional citizens to thrive, thereby projecting images of strength for the entire institution.

Activities

The Human Knot

Materials needed: none

This activity may be familiar to participants and is sometimes called the "Gordian knot" activity, referencing a Greek legend about Alexander the Great. The gist of the legend is that there was a wagon secured by ropes fastened in so many knots – so tangled and complicated – that the one who could accomplish the feat of freeing the wagon would be declared the ruler of the realm. In this activity, we use the title "human knot" so as to extend the story and experience beyond any historical, geographical, or cultural boundaries. This activity works well with groups of 8 to 12 people. Larger groups can be divided into smaller groups of this size.

1. The activity begins with group members standing in a circle, facing inward. Invite participants to close their eyes and reach/extend their arms into the center of the circle, clasping hands with someone else's extended hands. In a minute or so, everyone will have clasped hands with others and won't know whose hands they are holding and their position in the group until they open their eyes.
2. Once everyone's hands are linked with the hands of others, the group members can open their eyes.
3. The challenge now comes: the group must untangle themselves, forming a circle, without letting go of any hands. The group members can speak to each other, strategize, climb over and under each other, and may be facing a different direction when they end than when they began.
4. At the end of the activity, take a few moments to notice how the experience felt. What did people notice about the experience? Where

were there moments of pause, confusion, and/or leaps forward? What kinds of suggestions were helpful? Were there some ideas that were surprising? Some characteristics that emerged as strengths that are typically perceived differently?

Team and Team Again

Materials needed: none

This activity is designed for groups of people, ideally 15–20 or larger. The goal of the activity is for people to form a "team" according to directions that are provided by an instructions giver, or otherwise self-determined, accordingly.

1. The activity commences with the instructions giver calling out directions, such as "Form a team of four people" or "Form a team with three others whose first names begin with the same first letter as your first name" or any other specific instruction.
2. Participants then commence finding others in the group who meet the specifications. When the group is formed, the groups signal that they are "complete" by raising their hands, or sitting on the floor, or some other means of indicating that they are "done."
3. The instructions giver calls out additional directions for a few more rounds, including opportunities for individuals to form groups based on their own ideas (e.g., "form a team of four people"), and then, the members of the groups can share how they defined themselves as a group once all groups have been formed.
4. Once the whole activity is concluded, the large group can discuss strategies that were helpful throughout the activity, times they took leadership roles and times when they were happy to let others take the lead, and other noticings.

Paper Airplanes with a Twist

Materials needed: paper of various kinds, shapes, and sizes; tape; paper clips; markers, crayons, and/or stickers for decorating.

This activity works well with groups of any size. Smaller groups can engage in this activity with individuals making their own paper airplanes, and larger groups can collaborate on the paper airplane design and construction.

1. Each person or pair or cluster of participants is tasked with creating a paper airplane that they will take turns flying in front of the group.

2. People can share ideas about the different ways to construct paper airplanes. Some people may have done this many times and will have strong opinions about the "best" or "right" way to build the paper airplane, and others will have never tried this before.
3. Participants can experiment with different kinds of paper – different textures, weights, foldability – and can use tape and/or paper clips to assist with aerodynamics or aesthetics.
4. When everyone has had a chance to fly their plane, the group can provide positive and constructive feedback about the different designs. Model ways of commenting such as, "I like the way you used a paper clip at the front of the plane to guide it in the direction you wanted it to go," or "I wonder if you had folded the paper in half first, whether or not it would have flown farther?" Notice what strengths people point out, such as farthest, highest, most original design, most decorative, and so on, to emphasize how different ideas contribute to the group's overall understanding about paper airplanes, physics, teamwork, and more.

Digital Media

Culture Stew

https://msmglobalconsulting.com/category/culture-stew-podcast/

This site features blog posts and podcasts on a range of topics that explore race, gender, age, ethnicity, and other cultural groups distinguished by various factors. Originally at https://culturestew.me/, founder Maria Morukian is committed to examining human nature through lenses that promote greater awareness and appreciation for differences. The materials on this website support an inclusive environment that builds trust and utilizes citizens' strengths as assets.

Talking Inclusion – Podcast with Bill Armstrong

https://www.listennotes.com/podcasts/talking-inclusion-bill-armstrong-6ySqjzEp4oC/

This podcast series, produced and developed in Australia, features people and stories that open windows into others' lived experiences. The intent behind the podcast is a belief that sharing stories will contribute to greater empathy and understanding that will, in turn, reduce bias and increase human connection. The link above provides access to several episodes and descriptions for each one.

Teaching in Higher Ed Podcast

https://www.listennotes.com/podcasts/teaching-in-higher/transformative-inclusion-ki0XQAJfSOo/

This episode, "Transformative Inclusion," emphasizes a focus on strengths and systems. Bringing an educational context to the fore, Bill Eaton encourages listeners to consider people as more than just their behaviors or individual acts. How can environments integrate people's strengths and talents into a broader whole? What does it take to re-envision teaching and learning environments so that differences are welcome and not deficits?

Additional Resources

Intersectionality (Collins & Bilge, 2020)
The second edition of this highly regarded text by Patricia Hill Collins and Sirma Bilge presents the concept of intersectionality and explores how it provides a critical lens in academia (and elsewhere) through which to examine social inequalities and inequities. The authors present race, gender, ability, class, sexuality, and other identities as they not only describe but also apply concepts so that readers gain a better understanding of the relevance in their most immediate, intimate contexts as well as a global context. Keeping social justice at the core, the authors provide rich material for those new to the concept of intersectionality as well as to those who wish to extend their understanding and activism.

This Is Woman's Work (Christina, 2015)
Author and poet Dominique Christina writes, "To author ourselves, to own the expanse of our voices and our stories, is critical for us as women" (p. 3). In this book, Christina encourages readers to connect with their complex selves. She engages readers with poetry, provocative stories, and questions that prompt reflection and interaction, as readers learn more about themselves and their connections to and with others.

Universal Interconnectedness – Science and Spirituality

https://www.youtube.com/watch?v=lNVb4Aa1KmM

This video features Eckhart Tolle in conversation with Lothar Schafer, engaged in discussion about science and spiritual practice. Their discussion covers topics that are presented in a context that is inviting for non-scientists and novices interested in mindfulness and meditation, who might find other attempts to explain related concepts intimidating and confusing. As administrators and faculty members gain insights into how their work overlaps and intersects, they can better envision their efforts as aligned and interconnected. This awareness can contribute to greater capacity for understanding and empathy in the institution.

PRACTICE COMPASSION

The following materials have been selected because they represent efforts and intent on the part of the creators to explore our purpose in our respective roles and how we can develop. The skills that develop through listening experiences are applicable in myriad workplace situations and foster new ways of encountering people with opinions and experiences that differ from your own.

Activities

Culture in Academia

Materials needed: pen/pencil and notebook or digital note-taking tools (e.g., smartphone, tablet, laptop).

   This activity is designed for people to do individually, and this can also be completed/shared by individuals as members of small groups. The idea is that this activity will be done repeatedly, predictably, from time to time, so that people gain practice and familiarity with the elements that help them notice the dynamics in their institution that feel familiar, foreign, comfortable, uncomfortable, and more. The questions can be typed up and printed in multiple copies, carried in one's work bag or notebook, and therefore easily accessed for reflection during meetings or quiet times alone or with a few community members.

1. Is there a current or past situation in which you feel/felt disrespected? Is it possible that the situation involves a cultural priority that you hold dear?
2. Is there a current tension within your institution that might have a cultural priority at its core? In this situation, are you the party who feels misunderstood or the party who is misunderstanding someone/something else?
3. What do you see as the other party's priority in this situation? Who can be your guide to help you understand if your assumption about this priority is accurate?

4. What do you wish the other party understood about you or about what you value in this situation? Who can be your guide to help you understand what the other party wishes you knew about them?
5. What is at stake for you? Who can help you understand what is at stake for the other party?
6. Having conversations with others about your assumptions and perspectives in a specific situation does not guarantee that everyone will eventually reach consensus about anything. Yet, the act of seeking someone out and asking direct questions informs your own understanding and can reduce assumptions about other people and groups. This is a helpful first step toward building trust, so when disagreements or tensions inevitably arise, you understand some cultural values that are informing perceptions and behaviors.

Compassion Collages

Materials needed: magazines, several pairs of scissors, glue and/or scotch tape, large pieces of paper or poster board.

This activity is designed for small groups to work together on one group collage per group, though it can also be done with individuals creating their own collages that are shared and discussed with others.

1. Distribute materials among groups, so that each group (or individual) has one piece of large paper/poster board and access to magazines, scissors, and glue/tape. Invite participants to cut or rip images and/or words from magazines that reflect one specific feeling, as determined by the group.
2. Participants will co-construct a collage that represents the feeling, and when the collages are all complete, the finished work can be displayed in the room – on the walls or lying flat on tables – so that participants can walk around the room and take a few minutes to look at each collage.
3. When everyone has looked at all of the others' collages, then participants from each group can take turns sharing their individual or group collage. Once someone has spoken about one particular piece, then others participating in the activity can ask questions to clarify or learn more about the feeling collage (e.g., how they defined the feeling) and make connections or associations with some

of the images. Each individual or group takes a turn sharing what they are comfortable sharing.
4. People can take their collages and place them in shared spaces or leave them in a space to which they will return for future activities and conversations.

Lines Can Connect and Divide

Materials needed: masking tape or string that can be used on the floor; pieces of paper on which participants write when prompted; writing tools (e.g., pencils, pens).

This activity is designed for groups of 15–20 participants and is flexible for smaller and larger groups.

1. Begin by creating a line that divides floor space so that participants are standing on either side of the line, accordingly. Explain to the group that people can participate to the extent that they feel comfortable sharing with each other, and that this is a judgment-free zone.
2. Invite participants to write one thing that they think makes them unique, vulnerable, or strong (e.g., "I can run a marathon," "I had my appendix out," or "I am adopted"). The pieces of paper are collected by a designated instructions giver, who holds them and proceeds to read them out, one at a time.
3. The instructions giver directs participants to divide themselves on either side of the line and stand a few steps away from the tape/string line on the floor.
4. The instructions giver reads out one of the statements and pauses for a few moments, while participants who feel that the statement applies to them move closer to the line. The degree of closeness that people move correlates with the degree to which the statement applies to them. For example, if the statement is, "I am afraid of spiders," then participants who feel terrified of spiders might move right next to the line, while those who are only mildly disgusted by spiders take a small step toward the line. Precision isn't as important as noticing similarities among participants' feelings and experiences.
5. After a few rounds of this movement toward and away from the line, the group can gather together for some brief reflection. How did they feel sharing something new about themselves? Did sharing make them feel stronger or more vulnerable? What types of items were more difficult to admit, compared with others? Other questions and pondering are welcome. Participants may also enjoy writing or sketching before they discuss with the larger group.

Digital Media

Lee Mun Wah – The Secret to Changing the World

https://www.youtube.com/watch?v=Hp5SNpCtiWk

This YouTube video presents a TEDx Expression College talk given by Lee Mun Wah. The author, filmmaker, educator, and Asian folkteller shares accounts of some childhood experiences feeling like an "other," as well as more recent interactions with people that have afforded opportunities for growth and compassion, getting to know the other. He argues that if everyone could welcome opportunities to learn with and about other people's ways of being, the world would be a stronger, more compassionate place.

Deeya Khan – White Right: Meeting the Enemy

https://deeyah.com/blog/white-right-meeting-enemy/

In this award-winning documentary, filmmaker Deeya Khan engages White men – members of racist, "alt-right" movements – in candid, direct conversations about racism in the United States and the ideology that underpins their actions. Throughout the film, conversations exemplify how communication can lead to understanding of "the other" (a.k.a., the "enemy") and empathy.

Diana Chapman Walsh – Opening Keynote Address at the International Symposium for Contemplative Studies (ISCS) Mind & Life Institute 2014

https://www.mindandlife.org/insight/iscs-2014-opening-keynote-diana-chapman-walsh/

In this keynote address, Diana Chapman Walsh lauds the "purpose, possibility, and promise" that the institute presents to participants. She cautions that there is a present risk confronting us – risk of losing the sense of what it means to be human. She encourages participants to recognize our interdependence, connections with the natural world, and so many issues that plague society. Through greater awareness and connection, she contends that greater potential for compassion will be possible.

Additional Resources

Three Insights About Compassion, Meditation, and the Brain

https://greatergood.berkeley.edu/article/item/three_insights_from_the_frontiers_of_the_mind

The Greater Good Science Center at University of California, Berkeley "studies the psychology, sociology, and neuroscience of well-being, and teaches skills that foster a thriving, resilient, and compassionate society." This article by Simon-Thomas (2012) presents major take-aways and links to additional resources inspired by presentations at the inaugural International Symposium for Contemplative Studies. The website in which this article is nestled holds a wealth of additional information that will inspire continued reflection and practice in your own institution.

The Dalai Lama Center for Ethics and Transformative Values

https://thecenter.mit.edu/home/mission/

This Center, based at the Massachusetts Institute of Technology (MIT) in Cambridge, MA, includes in its mission statement a dedication "to inquiry, dialogue, and education on the ethical and humane dimensions of life." The Center was founded to reflect and extend the vision of the 14th Dalai Lama, co-creating interdisciplinary efforts around the world. As you explore this site and learn about resources and efforts that can inspire practices in your institution, you may find the Transformative Teachers Collection of particular interest. Designed to promote "resilience and ethical leadership skills among young people," the resources can be instructive tools for any environment seeking to examine its own capacity for empathy and ethics.

The Transformative Effects of Mindful Self-Compassion

https://www.mindful.org/the-transformative-effects-of-mindful-self-compassion/

This article serves as the final recommended resource in our collection and a starting point for readers to begin an intentional practice of self-compassion. As the authors, Dr. Kristin Neff and Dr. Christopher Germer, describe, humans are often critical of themselves and not used to opening space for caring and embracing of our own experiences, thoughts, and feelings. Nurturing a practice of self-compassion, particularly for people who work in academic environments that can already be sources of tension and conflict, can be a priority. This type of practice can help administrators and faculty members lower their stress responses and tune in to their own wellbeing. This can, in turn, de-escalate emotions and focus collaborative energy on the overall health of the institution. This work begins with caring for one's self, coming back to one's center.

CONCLUSION

Most people report experiencing a similar sensation when returning home after travelling abroad: "It's good to be home." Taking time to travel – for work or vacation – affords opportunities to live among people with different customs, languages, clothing, foods, values, and perspectives. Such travels also make clear how many fundamental human qualities are shared, in spite of boundaries and vernacular, connecting us in ways that we may not otherwise know or believe to be true.

Just as we would prepare if we were planning to visit a different place, excited to learn about a different culture, administrators and faculty members can build bridges and strengthen their understandings about each other by proactively identifying some resources:

- Someone to serve as a guide to help us get to know them as individuals and as members of a socio-cultural group
- Someone to serve as a translator to help us understand and learn the language and communicate clearly
- Someone to help us understand the currency – what matters to people, what do they value, what is at stake for them.

The more that members of cultural groups in institutions of higher education learn about the other – across disciplines, across roles, and across pay grades – the more they will build familiarity that contributes to building blocks of trust in the academic community. It sounds simple, yet it is in itself a cultural shift that requires people to break out of traditional patterns and "silos" that keep people apart. The survival of any institution is in everyone's interest and the highest priority. Even if that priority is latent, it is still present as one that motivates all employees and contributes to the resilience of institutions over periods of years that span decades, even centuries:

> The resilience is attributable in part to the enduring attraction of a college education and to the absence of viable alternatives. Yet the survival of universities is chiefly due to their capacity to reform themselves. The question is whether this demonstrated capacity to adapt is sufficiently elastic to overcome the current range, intensity, magnitude, and complexity of the threats.
>
> (Paquette, 2021, p. 32)

It is this very motivation that has inspired the authors of this book to engage in the work and the research that we have been committed to for decades, and that we share with you in the hopes that you find these tools useful in your own environments. Our collaborative work grew out of a trusting relationship that evolved over years of meetings, conversations, and social occasions, inside and in addition to university events.

Our experience aligns with the wisdom often shared by globally renowned CEO Warren Buffett. Buffett has been interviewed many times over the years regarding the secrets of organizational success and survival, and people look to him for wisdom that can help them be more successful in their workplaces. One quality that he notes as important is that successful individuals "say no to spending time with uninspiring, critical, or negative people who drag them down. Time is precious – choose a small circle of people who will energize you and challenge you to be better (Schwantes, 2018, par. 10)."

Administrators and faculty members have been working alongside each other in academia since the 1200s, perhaps longer. The tensions that have existed throughout the centuries have contributed to stereotypes and perceptions of the other like the following, penned by Benjamin Ginsberg (2013), author and professor of Political Science at Johns Hopkins University. Regarding faculty, he admits that "[p]rofessors, taken as a group, are far from perfect. They can be petty, foolish, venal, lazy, and quarrelsome" (p. 201). Of administrators, Ginsberg notes:

> University administrators aping last year's management argot provide comic relief for the faculty, but their underlying purpose is not amusing. What all management theories have in common is an effort to impose order and hierarchy on an institution. Even those theories that provide a place for employee involvement see this as a way of pacifying underlings with the appearance of consultation. Through their management speak, administrators are asserting that the university is an institution to be ruled by them.
>
> (p. 208)

These excerpts are quips that may resonate with academic community members, who recognize self and others in the descriptions. Yet, the act of writing a book provides one-way communication, and the act of reading a book provides readers with, at best, retention and application. Neither of these acts is as transformative as dialogue with others who are invested in the work. We sincerely hope that this book provides you with tools that open the door to some important conversations – ones that sustain and inform your professional and personal journey.

SUMMARY

Tensions between administrators and faculty members are predictable, to be sure, and there are strategies that can be utilized to strengthen relationships and build trust in academic communities. There are, however, some situations that are too toxic and therefore too unhealthy for someone to be able to thrive. Activities and resources designed to deepen listening, promote inclusion, and develop compassion are provided, which will empower institutional citizens to act and reflect, as individuals and members of the broader community culture.

REFERENCES

Christina, S. (2015). *This is woman's work: Calling forth your inner council of wise, brave, crazy, rebellious, loving, luminous selves.* Sounds True.

Collins, P.H., & Bilge, S. (2020). *Intersectionality* (2nd ed.). Polity Press.

Flaherty, C. (2017, April 21). Aftermath of a professor's suicide. *Inside Higher Ed.* Retrieved at https://www.insidehighered.com/news/2017/04/21/recent-suicide-professor-sparks-renewed-discussions-about-access-mental-health

Ginsberg, B. (2013). *The fall of the faculty.* Oxford University Press.

Masten, A.S. (2014). *Ordinary magic: Resilience in development.* The Guilford Press.

Paquette, G. (2021, April 2). Can higher ed save itself? Business as usual won't solve the existential challenges we face. Will anything? *The Chronicle of Higher Education,* 67(15), 32–37.

Rinaldi, C. (2001, Fall). The pedagogy of listening: The listening perspective from Reggio Emilia. *Innovations in Early Education: The International Reggio Exchange,* 8(4), 1–4.

Russo, R. (1997). *Straight man.* Vintage Books.

Sabina, L.L. (2021, January). Toxic Friday: Resources for addressing faculty bullying in higher education. *Journal of Faculty Development,* 35(1), 79–81.

Schwantes, M. (2018, January 18). Warren Buffett says this one simple habit separates successful people from everyone else. *Inc.* Retrieved at https://www.inc.com/marcel-schwantes/warren-buffett-says-this-is-1-simple-habit-that-separates-successful-people-from-everyone-else.html

Seltzer, R. (2016, July 8). A president's suicide. *Inside Higher Ed.* Retrieved at https://www.insidehighered.com/news/2016/07/08/texas-am-commerce-president-committed-suicide

Simon-Thomas, E.R. (2012). Three insights about compassion, meditation, and the brain. *Mind & Body.* Retrieved at https://greatergood.berkeley.edu/article/item/three_insights_from_the_frontiers_of_the_mind

Sipress, D. (2009, April 20). Daddy works in a magical, faraway land called Academia. *The New Yorker.* Conde Nast.

Sternberg, R. (2019, October 1). A theory of adaptive intelligence and its relation to general intelligence. *Journal of Intelligence,* 7(23), 1–17.

Stripling, J. (2017, July 21). How one leader set a toxic tone, spurning allies she needed most. *The Chronicle of Higher Education,* 63(41), A13–A17.

Index

Note: **Bold** page numbers refer to tables and *italic* page numbers refer to figures.

academia: BIPOC community members in 143–144; and business 103–104; women in 142–143
academic freedom 31
academic robes 135–136
academics and college experience 104–106
Academic Senate 27–28
acceptance 71
accessibility: administrator perspectives 49–50; faculty perspectives 48–49; higher education 47–50; quality and quantity 47–48
accountability: as element of inclusive leadership 164; and institutions of higher education 117
adaptation 71; and exit 171–172
administration 23; administrator perspective 28–30; complex notion of power 35–36; cultural groups 22–23; healthy dose of discourse 23–28; transparency 34–35; tuning in 21–22; weighing the risks of vulnerability 35

administrator perspectives 28–30; governance 116–117; higher education 46–47; resources 84–85; territory 98–99; tradition 131–132; trust 158
administrators 29–30; archetypes 11–12; frustrations 30; privileges 29–30; tradition 139; transparency and privacy 34–35; validation 30; vulnerabilities 29
aesthetics and appearance 134
American Association of University Professors (AAUP) 8
American Association of University Women (AAUW) 142
American College President Study 30
American Council on Education (ACE) 134, 135–136
American Sign Language 45
appearance and aesthetics 134
Apple 44
Arizona State University 134
The Art of Dialogue 177
Asian culture 68
assistant professor 26
associate professor 26
The Atlantic (Bogost) 105

191

INDEX

authenticity 159
awareness and higher education 65–66

Ballenger, J. 143
BBC News 112
beliefs about programs 9–10
Berlin Wall, fall of 42
Bilge, Sirma: *Intersectionality* 181
BIPOC community members in academia 143–144
A Bit of Optimism Podcast – Extreme Listening 176
Black, Indigenous, and People of Color (BIPOC) 56, 142, 153
Black Lives Matter protests 117
Bode, P. 8
Bogost, Ian: *The Atlantic* 105
boundary: between academics and college experience 104–106; between business and academia 103–104
Boyer, Ernest: *We Must Find New Forms for Higher Education* 41–42
"brick and mortar" buildings 47
Buffett, Warren 188
business and academia 103–104
Byram, M. 66

Cambridge 105, 134
case study: governance 112–114; resources 81–83; territory 95–97; tradition 129–131; trust 154–156
The Center for American Progress 87
ceremonial mace 135
chain of office 135
chancellor 24
Christensen, Clay 43
Christina, Dominique: *This Is Woman's Work* 181
The Chronicle of Higher Education 40, 87, 151
Cohen, A. 161
collaborative communication 163

collaborative research 12–13
collective bargaining agreements (CBAs) 27
Collins, Patricia Hill: *Intersectionality* 181
comfort in conflict 68
commencement festivities 129–131
communication 8; collaborative 163; consistent 88; higher education 65–66; institutional 119; intercultural 8, 13–15, 23, 27, 57, 61–62, 66–71, 73, 91, 140, 160, 163, 169, 172; intergroup 48
compassion 165–166, 169–170, 182–186; activities 182–184; additional resources 185–186; Compassion Collages 183–184; Culture in Academia 182–183; The Dalai Lama Center for Ethics and Transformative Values 186; digital media 185; Lines Can Connect and Divide 184; *Three Insights About Compassion, Meditation, and the Brain* 185–186; *The Transformative Effects of Mindful Self-Compassion* 186
competence and higher education 65–66
competency 159
conflict: comfort in 68; interpersonal 108–109; navigating 4–6; socially co-constructed 16; territorial 94
congruency 159
consistent communication 88
context: governance in 117–120; territory in 100–103; tradition in 133–139; trust in 158–161
convocation 136–137
corruption and trust 153–157
Cosmopolitan 31
courage, as element of inclusive leadership 164

INDEX

COVID-19 pandemic 3, 40, **41**, 42, 45, 52, 87, 90, 100, 105–106, 113, 120, 164; lockdown 103
Crawford, Joan 130
critical race feminism (CRF) 143
critical race theory (CRT) 143
"cross-cultural" 7
cultural context 85–88; administrators' concerns 86–88; faculty members' concerns 86; students' concerns 85–86
cultural currency 15, 88–90
cultural groups 22–23
cultural imperative 151–166
cultural norms 67–68; comfort in conflict 68
cultural priority 79–91, 94–107, 110–124, 127–144; and trust 173
cultural successes 90–91
cultural universals 90–91; cultural successes 90–91
culture 6–7; Asian 68; collective 68; individual 68; institutional 13, 100; Western 68, 111
Curzon-Hobson, A. 159
cutting-edge consortium 154–156

The Dalai Lama Center for Ethics and Transformative Values 186
dean 25
Deardorff, D.K. 66, 67
Decolonization is not a Metaphor (Tuck and Yang) 137
denial 70
Denisova-Schmidt, E. 156, 165
dependability 159
descriptive norms 67
The Developing Mind (Siegel) 162–163
Diana Chapman Walsh – Opening Keynote Address at the International Symposium for Contemplative Studies (ISCS) Mind & Life Institute 2014 185

Difficult Dialogues Initiative at Clark University 177
digital media 176–177, 180–181, 185; *A Bit of Optimism Podcast – Extreme Listening* 176; *Culture Stew* 180; Opening Keynote Address at the International Symposium for Contemplative Studies (ISCS) Mind & Life Institute 2014 185; *The Secret to Changing the World* 185; StoryCorps 176; *Talking Inclusion – Podcast with Bill Armstrong* 180; *Teaching in Higher Ed Podcast* 181; *White Right: Meeting the Enemy* 185; *Why It's Worth Listening to People You Disagree With* 176–177
diplomas 138
discourses 23–28
"disruptive innovation" 43
diversity 8
Drawing Duos (activity) 174–175
Dzurek, D.J. 98, 107

empowerment as element of inclusive leadership 164
environmental toxins, resilience and risks 170–172
European Union 42
exclusion, traditions of 142–144
exit and adaptation 171–172

face-to-face instruction 43–45
faculty 25; archetypes 11
Faculty Assembly 27–28
faculty members 31–33; frustrations 33; privileges 32; tradition 138–139; validation 33–34; vulnerabilities 32
faculty member's perspective 31–34; governance 115–116; higher education 45–46; resources 83–84; territory 99–100; tradition 132–133; trust 157–158

193

INDEX

fairness 159
Floyd, George 54, 73, 137
Forbes magazine 159
foreign currency 89–90
Fox, Christine 35
frustrations: administrator 30; faculty member 33

Gallos, J.V. 62
Galloway, Scott 44, 51
Gannon, K. 137
Germer, Christopher 186
Ginsberg, Benjamin 188
global fitness 69; developing 69
GlobalPeople initiative 69
gonfalons 135
Goodman, P. 80
Google 44
governance 8–9, 110–124; administrators' concerns 119–120; administrator's perspective 116–117; case study 112–114; in context 117–120; faculty members' concerns 118–119; faculty member's perspective 115–116; sharing is hard 122–124; student's concerns 118; time and tide wait for no institution 110–115; as tug-of-war 120–122
governing through uncertainty 112–114
Great Recession of 2008 40
Gupta, Sanjay 44

Hallman, K. 20
Hardin, Garrett 80
The Harvard Business Review 40
Henry VIII 134
higher education: accessibility matters 47–50; administrator perspectives 46–47; awareness, competence, and communication 65–66; faculty perspectives 45–46; fighting for survival 40–59; headlines **41**; identity matters 53–57; modality matters 43–45; money matters 50–53; no signal 41–43; online learning and face-to-face instruction 43–45; quality and quantity 47–48; racism and retention 54–55; re-envisioning the landscape 57; revenue generation and not-for-profit 51
higher education spending: administrator perspectives 52–53; faculty perspectives 51–52; revenue generation and not-for-profit 51
Historically Black Colleges and Universities (HBCUs) 143
HIV/AIDS 42
humility, as element of inclusive leadership 164

identity: administrator perspectives 56–57; faculty perspectives 55–56; higher education 53–57; racism and retention 54–55; tradition and 140–142
immunity to change 140
inclusion 24, 30, 53, 65, 114–115, 163–164, 178, 189
inclusive leadership 163–164, 178–182; activities 178–180; additional resources 181–182; digital media 180–181; The Human Knot 178–179; Paper Airplanes with a Twist 179–180; Team and Team Again 179
injunctive norms 67
institutional communication 119
institution and governance 110–115
instructor/lecturer 26
intercultural 7–8; communication 8, 13–15, 23, 27, 57, 61–62, 66–71, 73, 91, 140, 160, 163, 169, 172

INDEX

Intercultural Development Continuum 69–70
The Intercultural Development Inventory® (IDI ®) 69–70
intercultural (r)evolution: in practice 68–71; in theory 66–67
intercultural lenses 9–10; beliefs about programs 9–10; values embedded in programs 9
intergroup communication 48
Intersectionality (Collins and Bilge) 181
Isaacs, William 177

Jaffe, D. 159
Jain, N. 164
Jones, R.H. 7

Kegan, R. 140
Khan, Deeya: *White Right: Meeting the Enemy* 176, 185
Koverola, C. 9

Lahey, L.L. 140
leadership 28; practice inclusive 163–164, 178–182; women 64, 143
Lee Mun Wah: *The Secret to Changing the World* 185
Leung, A.S.M. 68
Levin, J.S. 100
life in the trenches 62–63
"linguistic collusion" 101
listening 4, 22–23, 61, 90, 161–163, 172–177; activities 173–176; additional resources 177; digital media 176–177; Drawing Duos 174–175; Listening – Inside and Out 173–174; repair 162–163; Word Play 175–176
Listening – Inside and Out (activity) 173–174
Lloyd, William Forster 80
Los Angeles Times 101

Made to Stick (Heath and Heath) 128
Massachusetts Institute of Technology (MIT) 177, 186
Masten, A.S. 170
Mbembe, A.J. 111
Middle Ages 135, 138
mindfulness 167, 181
minimization 70–71
modality, higher education 43–45
Mommie Dearest 130
money, and higher education 50–53
Morukian, Maria 180

Neff, Kristin 186
The New Yorker 169
The New York Times 112
Nieto, S. 8
norms 67; cultural 67–68; descriptive 67; injunctive 67
Northeastern University 140

Obama, Barack 42
O'Grady, K. 161–162
online instruction 95–97
online learning and face-to-face instruction 43–45
openness and vulnerability 159
organizational trust 152
other 5–6; cultivating capacity to understand perspective of 10–12, 72
Oxford 105, 134

The Pedagogy of Listening (Rinaldi) 177
personal trust 152
perspective: administrator 28–30, 46–47, 49–50, 52–53, 56–57, 84–85, 98–99, 116–117, 131–132, 158; faculty 31–34, 45–46, 48–49, 51–52, 55–56, 83–84, 99–100, 115–116, 132–133, 157–158; of the other 10–12

INDEX

Piller, I. 7, 22
plan for action 169–189
polarization 70
pomp and circumstance 134
power 35–36; complex notion of 35–36
president 23–24
privacy and administrators 34–35
privileges: administrator 29–30; faculty member 32
professor 26
programs: beliefs about 9–10; values embedded in 9
provost 24

racism and retention 54–55; higher education 54–55
reliability 159
research, collaborative 12–13
resilience and risks 170–172
resources 79–91; administrator's perspective 84–85; case study 81–83; cultural context 85–88; cultural currency 88–90; cultural universals 90–91; faculty member's perspective 83–84; under threat 79–83
Rinaldi, Carlina: *The Pedagogy of Listening* 177
risks: and resilience 170–172; of vulnerability 35
Roe v. Wade 42
Rosowsky, D.V. 20
Russo, Richard: *Straight Man* 11, 169
Rutgers University 87

Schafer, Lothar 181
science of tradition 128–131
Scollon, R. 7
Scollon, S.W. 7
sharing 122–124
Siegel, Daniel: *The Developing Mind* 162–163

Simon-Thomas, E.R.: *Three Insights About Compassion, Meditation, and the Brain* 185–186
sincerity 159
Sinek, Simon 176
Sipress, D. 169
Spencer-Oatey, Helen 61, 67, 69
Spiliakos, A. 80
Sternberg, R. 171–172
StoryCorps 176
Straight Man (Russo) 11, 169
strategic trust 152
Sulé, V.T. 53, 143
survival 40–58
syllabus 137

tassels 137–138
taxonomy of territory 94–98
tenure 26–27
territory 94–107; administrators' concerns 102–103; administrator's perspective 98–99; boundary between academics and college experience 104–106; boundary between business and academia 103–104; building trust has its benefits 106–107; case study 95–97; in context 100–103; faculty members' concerns 102; faculty member's perspective 99–100; students' concerns 101–102; taxonomy of 94–98
This Is Woman's Work (Christina) 181
Thorpe, J.R. 133
threat, resources under 79–83
Three Insights About Compassion, Meditation, and the Brain (Simon-Thomas) 185–186
Tolle, Eckhart 181
tradition 127–144; academic robes 135–136; administrators' concerns 139; administrator's perspective 131–132; appearance and aesthetics 134; case study

196

129–131; ceremonial mace 135; chain of office 135; in context 133–139; convocation 136–137; diplomas 138; of exclusion 142–144; faculty members' concerns 138–139; faculty member's perspective 132–133; gonfalons 135; and identity 140–142; immunity to change 140; pomp and circumstance 134; science of tradition 128–131; students' concerns 138; syllabus 137; tassels 137–138; and transformation 144

traditions of exclusion 142–144; BIPOC community members in academia 143–144; women in academia 142–143

transformation and tradition 144

The Transformative Effects of Mindful Self-Compassion 186

transparency 159; administrators 34–35

trust 151–166; administrators' concerns 161; administrator's perspective 158; building, and its benefits 106–107; case study 154–156; in context 158–161; corruption 153–157; and cultural priorities *173*; faculty members' concerns 160–161; faculty member's perspective 157–158; practice compassion 165–166; practice inclusive leadership 163–164; practice listening 161–163; students' concerns 160; trust detours 152–153; values that build *14*

trust detours 152–153

Tuck, E.: *Decolonization is not a Metaphor* 137

uncertainty and governance 112–114
unionization 27
union/non-union 27

United States Supreme Court 42
Universal Interconnectedness – Science and Spirituality 181–182
University of California, Berkeley 186
University of Coimbra 134
University of Paris 110
University of Warwick 69
University of Washington 135
U.S. Centers for Disease Control and Prevention 42

validation: administrator 30; faculty member 33–34
Välimaa, J. 151, 152
values: embedded in programs 9; that build trust *14*
"the Velcro theory of memory" 128
vice presidents/vice chancellors 24–25
vulnerabilities: administrator 29; faculty member 32; weighing the risks of 35

Walsh, Diana Chapman 177; Opening Keynote Address at the International Symposium for Contemplative Studies (ISCS) Mind & Life Institute 2014 185
We Must Find New Forms for Higher Education (Boyer) 41–42
Western culture 68, 111
White Right: Meeting the Enemy (Khan) 176, 185
Why It's Worth Listening to People You Disagree With 176–177
women: in academia 142–143; as consummate other 64–65; leadership 64, 143
Wood, Zachary R. 177
World War I 62

Yang, K.W.: *Decolonization is not a Metaphor* 137
Ylijoki, O. 151, 152

197